SPIRIT WORK

ABOUT AUTHOR

Sirian Shadow is a writer, psychic, and energy worker, and draws his spiritual influences and inspiration from many paths. First published in *A Harvest of Tales: An Anthology of Short Stories From Young Canadians* at the age of seventeen, he pursued an education with writing and majored in English at university. Changing course, he graduated with a diploma in graphic design, but continued his passion. Compelled to answer the call as a healer, he received certification in Usui Reiki and became an initiate of shamanism. He developed his psychic and mediumship skills through the Arthur Findlay College. With his developed skills and experience in the mystical arts, he is devoted to helping people open their eyes to the truth about themselves and the world around them.

Discover The Existence & Nature of Spirits

SPIRIT WORK

A Guide to Communicating
& Forming Relationships
with Spirits

SIRIAN SHADOW

Second Edition 2022

Book & design by Sirian Shadow
Cover Illustration by Vecteezy/Bayu Dwi Cahyono

Independently Published
Registered at Library and Archives Canada
Names: Shadow, Sirian
Title: Spirit Work: A Guide to Communicating & Forming Relationships with
    Spirits
Description: First edition. | Includes bibliographical references. | Summary:
    "Spirit Work is an introduction and guide to the magic of working with
    spirits. This book is written for the novice about spirit realms and the magic
    behind connecting to spirits such as spirit guides, ancestors, and deities; from
    identifying and communicating with them, to building and maintaining
    positive spiritual relationships. It also draws on the author's practical
    experience of developing beneficial relationships with spirits. Working with
    spirits is intrinsically a sacred art, but it's a practical one too. This book is
    intended to teach how to develop and improve meaningful and fulfilling
    relationships with spirits, and to help people understand and connect with
    the spiritual realms so they may be presented with the opportunity to learn
    more about energies and entities" —Provided by publisher.
Identifiers: ISBN 978-1-7780761-0-7 (paperback)
ISBN 978-1-7780761-5-2 (hardcover) ISBN 978-1-7780761-2-1 (ebook)

Acknowledgments
Without the support of the people in my life, I would not have been able to
write the book you are about to read. First and foremost, I want to express my
gratitude to my parents. Second, I'd like to express my gratitude to my friends
Michelle and Amanda, who have always supported me and encouraged me to
pursue my goals. I've discovered that the soul-bond we have is some of the most
powerful magic I've ever encountered. Finally, I'd like to express my gratitude to
the spirits of my ancestors and those of the land, as well as my guides and allies.

Other Books by Sirian Shadow
Charlie's Special Gift
The Witch's Coloring Book of Spells
The Journal For Magic
Earth and Bone Oracle Deck

To Artismus, my ally, guardian and companion on this journey of Spirit Work.

CONTENTS

INTRODUCTION

For each practitioner, belief and practice will vary. The practices, information, and exercises outlined in this book may provide examples in regard to religious sensibility; however, spirit work does not belong to any one religion. For this reason, the exercises and writings in this book are considered nondenominational, as most practitioners see this work as being inherently spiritual, even if they aren't a spiritual person in other aspects of their lives. Your beliefs should be your own, and this book does not claim that there is a master list to follow in order to achieve effective results from the knowledge and lessons shared here. Throughout your discovery of forming relationships and working with spirits, you will begin to understand that spirit work is really very personal. A word of advice: listen to yourself.

Although the label you associate with may vary, the general term I will refer to in this book is *practitioner*. Learning to work with spirits is a form of energy work that can be very much aligned with and part of magic. To be a practitioner of the work, you understand that it does not belong to any one group or social classification. And I'm not referring to the kind of magic that is associated with stage performance illusions or tricks for the amusement of others, but real magic—as in tapping in to supernatural energies and working with them for desired outcomes, a method of influencing our physical reality through metaphysical means by ways of ritual practice. I'll discuss more about what magic is and how understanding it has helped me connect more meaningfully to spirits, but for now, understand that this book is intended for positive knowledge and practicality that can be beneficial for everyone.

Each practitioner's level of competency will vary depending on a person's skills, gifts, abilities, experiences, commitment, and foundations of their practice. How a practitioner identifies, interacts, and works with the spirits they choose will also play a vital role in progression and development. Practices vary, just like their administrators, and so as an author and practitioner I can only share the information or give insight about the fundamentals and theories of my own practice. Two authors might write about their spiritual practice and come up with two very different experiences and interpretations. It is, therefore, up to you to consider and take into account what you connect with and disregard that which you do not. Spirit work is not, nor ever will be, a one-size-fits-all practice. It is heavily influenced by your experiences. That is why this book can only go so far. The rest is up to you to put the theory and exercises to use and measure what is or isn't effective based on your individual perceptions.

It's foolish to think that there is one simple method that will lead you to effectively and efficiently cultivate working relationships with spirits. The truth is, all forms of spiritual communication take time to develop, including: channeling, mediumship, divination, and meditation. There isn't an easy or quick way to access spiritual realms without first understanding how to do so and what that personal experience is like. And just like a skilled vocalist, although they may have been born with gifts and talents, reaching a certain level of proficiency takes time, effort, and due diligence. There is no simple, quick, or straightforward technique to quickly provide you the ability to converse and work with spirits, and there never has been. You may begin to enhance your talents through time, effort, and knowing more about the approaches you are drawn to and interested in. Don't be afraid to try everything; there is not a singular or simple path to becoming an expert. Just like in all subjects, there are many ways to learn, study, and become proficient.

Before diving into spirit work, a word of advice—fear has no place in spirit work, so if you are hesitant or fearful, don't be. This book is intended to give you more assurance to be confident in working with spirits. Although for any practitioners who have committed to this practice, they understand that they are not invincible. We understand that light cannot exist without dark, and as a practitioner, when you follow your spiritual path you must first understand that we are a part of a world of both positive and negative entities, energies, and events. Be aware that both sides can affect us, but we are powerful and capable of setting boundaries.

If you still feel hesitant and fearful by the time you are done reading this, maybe reconsider if spirit work is for you. Not every practitioner needs to seek the aid of spirits, and many do just fine manipulating energies and benefitting without them. However, I would not be who I am without my relationships with my spirit allies, nor would I have developed an understanding of the universe without exploration of this sacred art. Spirit work can be tremendously rewarding if you allow it.

Before beginning spirit work, ask yourself what your intentions are for learning it. Believing wholeheartedly in the work will most certainly provide more positive and incredible results. If you don't fully commit, then the results will be directly tied to your efforts and will be less than significant. In other words, believing is seeing. Skepticism will prevent anyone from achieving their full potential and the best results.

Allow me to be clear on what this book is not. This book is not intended to teach you how to use spirits to provide entertainment for others. Spiritualists are also empiricists. This means that they learn from their experiences, by working and practicing while holding space for personal development or a calling to heal and be in service for others. The work is adaptable and versatile. A book alone will not give you the validating experiences of psychic abilities in all its theories. The work comes down to you and your intention to do no harm. Although psychic ability will be improved as a result of performing the exercises, and if followed correctly, you will experience tremendous results and connections with spirits.

However, this book is not intended to teach newly strengthened abilities to show off. The truth is that if your intentions are less than honorable, you will not be able to develop and utilize the skills in the way you might hope, and you may need to re-examine why you feel drawn to spirit work. It's been proven that positive intentions, in combination with love, have far greater outcomes in learning to work with spirits.

Spirit work is intrinsically a sacred art, but it's a practical one too. Moreover, this book is intended to teach you how to develop and improve meaningful and fulfilling relationships with spirits. The intention with this book is to help you understand and connect with other realms so you may be presented with the opportunity to understand more about energies and entities, and potentially attain beneficial spirit allies, if you so choose.

It's important to understand that authors who write on the subject of spiritual development or spirit work are not to be held accountable or responsible for any conditions that can occur along your path, as you are the creator of your life. Although development of these practices can be interesting and helpful, please use common sense and adhere to safety for your own sake. In other words, you reap what you sow—both positive and negative. You will find a section in the book that briefly discusses protective methods. Psychic or spiritual protection is nothing more than safeguarding, as we are already energetically and spiritually protected. As long as your intentions are to work from a place of compassion or the greatest good for all, then you needn't worry. Be assured, the exercises and information in this book are safe. However, if the subject of spiritual protection makes you feel uneasy, then I suggest you learn and familiarize yourself with what protection actually means before attempting spiritual practices.

Once a practitioner is comfortable with understanding and can comprehend their own boundaries and beliefs, speak their truth, and is not doubtful or fearful of entering and maintaining relationships with spirits, they are ready to dive deeper into their journey with spirits. It would be wise to document your experiences in a personal notebook or journal. The topics and exercises discussed in this book can be effective, but only if the practitioner is attuned to and understanding of their own experiences, and therefore capable of replicating them.

What works for some practitioners may not always work for others, which is why this practice is intrinsically a personal one. Many people can learn these techniques, but ultimately, the most difficult technique to ascertain is comprehending the concept of surrender and inner knowing—they must be attained by the practitioner individually. Ultimately, mastering abilities or skills is about practicing according to your experiences.

Chapter 1

PREPARING FOR SPIRIT
INTERACTIONS

We all have the choice to cocreate with spirits, and may use techniques and abilities to channel their power. In order to get in touch with those abilities and techniques, we first need to form an understanding of the perception and composition of our reality—to see spirits for what they are and how they communicate. Ceremonial magician and author Lon Milo DuQuette refers to the labels we give spirits, such as angels, demons, fairies, and so on, as metaphors.[1] While I agree that we employ metaphors to describe spirits in literary terms, spirits are made up of energy; therefore, what is the nature of that energy?

Practitioners who work with spirits know and understand that everything is composed of energy. Although we often measure energy with our five senses, we know, based on scientific measurements, that invisible energies exist. By scientific standards, radiant energy is a form of electromagnetic energy. It can take the form of visible waves, which is what we call light energy.

Other forms of invisible energetic waves exist too, such as radio waves or X-rays. The energy of electromagnetic waves can travel through space, and waves that transmit radiant energy come in all different forms. Light waves

---

1. DuQuette, Lon Milo, *Low Magick: It's All in Your Head, You Just Have No Idea How Big Your Head Is* (Woodbury, MN: Llewellyn Publications, 2010), 23.

are the only type of this energy we can see with our eyes. So you can see, energy is not limited to what we can see or measure with our five senses, as we're constantly interacting with energy that is invisible to us.

If invisible energy such as radiant energy exists that we can measure, then logically other forms of invisible energy also exist, including subtle or psychic energy. It can be sensed everywhere and comes in many forms—in people, places, objects, and animals. It exists all around us. A specific site, area, room, or building may give off certain vibrations or energies. We use our psychic senses to measure these energies. These energies may be sensed and detected by those who are in touch with their psychic abilities and intuition. Like the energy of a specific site, area, or place, these invisible energies also include but are not limited to auras, internal body (circuit) energy, object energy, energetic messages, and entities.

All life-forms radiate energy fields. Some practitioners believe that human energetic fields or auras are more complex because of our evolutionary existence. Auras have been witnessed and studied for centuries. Some practitioners have assigned colors for their varied meanings. Their colors are linked to the body's seven chakras, or psychic-energy centers, which are important in Hinduism and Buddhism. The seven chakras consist of the root chakra at the base of the spine and is associated with the color red. The sacral chakra is located below the navel and is associated with orange. The solar plexus chakra is located at the stomach and is yellow. The heart chakra is located at the center of the chest and is green. The throat chakra at the center of the neck is a light blue. The third eye chakra is located between the eyebrows and is a dark purple. The crown chakra at the top of the head is magenta or white.

The aura is a three-dimensional energy field that surrounds the body. It is influenced by the physical body's energy field. When we harmonize our senses and open ourselves to all of the subtle energies within us, we can begin to experience the positive influence of the spirit realm. The stronger and more balanced our auric field is, the more easily it can be tuned to all of the subtle influences within life.[2]

---

2. Andrews, Ted, *How To Meet and Work With Spirit Guides*, 2nd ed (Woodbury, MN: Llewellyn Publications, 2006), 36.

Energies that make up spirits or entities tend to be denser than that of the milder life force energies. Their energy is simply moving at a different vibrational frequency or speed. Understanding the varied kinds of energy helps practitioners differentiate them. We refer to them as psychic, subtle, or invisible energies because they cannot be measured or deciphered with the use of the five senses.

Very few people realize the tremendous influences that the invisible world has on our everyday lives because we are often so focused on the visible or physical world. Many people have been falsely conditioned into believing that only the observable, tangible, and sensory world exists and that everything else outside of it must be nonexistent or purely imaginary. This belief has led to the suppression of the senses that detect and filter energies that are unseen. The truth is, our psychic abilities can detect and interact with an abundance of invisible energy. The abilities to filter, detect, and interact with invisible energies often need to be strengthened—they are not altogether gone but are already within us, ready to be awakened.

The reason that so many people ignore the invisible energies is because most try to measure and detect them with only the five physical senses and therefore cannot discern these energies because they do not have a developed system to do so. We as practitioners understand that our bodies are tools, capable of measuring and filtering all kinds of energy and information.

The majority of people don't even realize when they've made contact with spirits. Spirits can appear in as many forms as there are spirits. They have been known to appear as light orbs, shadows, or other subtle forms of energy. They can be recognized by any of our psychic senses and our bodies. Some people may encounter them with psychic senses in the form of beings, colors, animals, or symbols, and for others, they may appear to us in dreams or other planes of consciousness.

So how do we know if we encounter a spirit or if it's just in our minds? It all comes down to relying on our intuition and removing our logical minds from the experience. If we can develop the awareness to recognize when our brain isn't responsible for an experience—meaning, we didn't control it based on our beliefs, fears, or desires, and we feel it in our bones, like a gut feeling or instinct as confirmation, it's highly likely that you had a spiritual experience.

The degrees of spirit perception and interpretation vary according to a person's skills and abilities. There are several psychic senses referred to as the clairs or clair senses, but before diving into developing and understanding the psychic senses, the most important attribute needed in spirit work is a strong connection and awareness of our intuition. Developing the connection with our intuition is a simple process that anyone can do. However, doubting intuition with things like constant second-guessing can limit it, and will require much more practice and effort for someone to develop their abilities. If doubting is the case, a practitioner must learn to trust their experiences and remove their logical mind from the equation. In order to effectively communicate with spirits, we must engage our creative and imaginative part of the brain.

Western societal beliefs often have people relying on thinking with the left side of the brain and to dismiss things that seem like nonsense or made up. To become proficient in spirit work we must learn to, in a way, become daydreamers again. Psychic skill and advancement have been directly linked to the ability to let the imagination lead and silence the logical mind. For many—especially those who have been conditioned by societal beliefs to stop dreaming, so to speak—they will require extra persistence to re-examine their beliefs and establish newfound ideas.

Almost everyone has had an experience where they have detected spirits—whether they were conscious of it or not. These experiences are often categorized as supernatural or mystical. In reality, it's your body working as an energy detection system. Some pass off this detection as déjà vu, others may have had prophetic dreams or have had visions. Sometimes, people experience a strange feeling or inkling to trust their gut and instincts. Whatever these experiences are categorized as, it doesn't make them any less real. Trust them!

The skills to interact with spirits can be learned, but some people are born with gifts that give them the predisposition of being an effective practitioner. Those gifts are when a person is more adept at monitoring and filtering energy and then capable of deciphering what it's doing. Practitioners also have the ability to tap into and manipulate these energetic vibrations for desired outcomes and effects. By developing your skills for extrasensory perception, you can gain access to the spiritual world and therefore perceive these otherwise invisible energies.

Intuitive development is where most psychics or mediums begin to attune to these energies, and it's a skill that can be achieved by anyone (remember, these abilities are simply dormant in most people, not altogether gone). Through practice of development, it can be strengthened like an athlete training for a marathon. Practitioners are like athletes, in a way. A practitioner's abilities can be strengthened as a result of working on them and is done so by ironing out their negative habits, emotions, traumas, memories, and hidden aspects of their subconscious mind. A practice commonly referred to as shadow work—where these issues are brought to the surface and worked on to heal or accept, through things like meditation, affirmation, or psychotherapy—allows for a reprogramming of often deep-rooted subconscious blocks.

Another way in which intuitive development can be strengthened is through energy work such as reiki, yoga, or tai chi.[3] If you are looking to connect with spirits and do not have the foundational development for intuitive abilities, it can be much more challenging to make contact, trust your senses, form relationships, and be able to effectively communicate. In order to understand what those connections are and how to form them, you must first understand the importance of those energies and the energy that flows within you. Once your blockages are released and your intuition is strengthened, you will be well on your way to connecting with spirits and energies.

So, how do people ultimately connect with or communicate with spirits? I like to think of people as types of beacons or transmitters that are capable of not only generating and transmitting energetic waves, but also

---

3. Nathaniel, *The Art of Seeing Your Psychic Intuition, Third Eye, and Clairvoyance: A Practical Manual for Learning and Improving Your Clairvoyant Abilities* (Wrocław, Poland: A State of Mind, 2012), 10.

to perceive them once they are attuned. In order to perceive these energies and to access the different states of consciousness, we must practice. Imagine that it's like having control over a lever that opens or closes the floodgates at a dam. Once we are capable of perceiving energies, we can then begin to interpret them.

In large part, communication with spirits comes down to intuitive and psychic perception and development, but the methods to communicate vary. If you don't have inherent or innate abilities, then you have to put the work in to develop them. Without practice and development, you could be operating like a radio on the wrong channel—you won't be able to hear or understand the message until you adjust to the correct frequency. To begin, we must start with how to make sure your radio works, that it is on the right channel, and is transmitting clearly.

THE WORK: A RELATIONSHIP OF MAGIC, SPIRITS, AND ENERGY

Practitioners understand that all energy is connected and that we can tap into any energy, so let's examine the idea of internal symbiosis and relationships with energy. When people talk about spirits, deities, or these types of energies, some people choose to accept that the energy of entities is within them and is them—essentially believing that Source is inside of them and, therefore, they are of Source, Spirit, the Creator, God, or whatever name you choose to refer to it as. To assist in better understanding the energy that is the Creator, think of it as more of a web-like network of energy that cannot be personified with gender or as a face in the sky. We must understand that divinity does not maintain the human-like qualities or personifications people have often identified it with. Its power is expansive and beyond comprehension, and the core of that power is love. Some people choose to believe divinity exists as several beings in polytheistic traditions or as a singular being in monotheistic religions.

Source, God, divinity, or whatever term you want to call it, the universe is like a vast ocean, and we are only a small portion of it. As a result, we are divinity of divinity. All energy and beings are a part of that ocean, and we can use an irrigation system to connect to it. However, we would drown if we were to dive right into it, yet each irrigation system can filter a stream to fulfill an intent.

In other words, all pathways lead to source because everything is connected, and it is simpler to connect with aspects of source rather than its vastness. It's all related, and all elements of source are ultimately source, so it doesn't matter how you acquire your intention. It's all the same and produces the same outcome.

To connect and receive from the universe or source, we must transform ourselves into a valve that can appropriately filter the type of water we desire. So the aspects of source are often personified to help form a relationship and understand exchanges of things like love, honor, and veneration. This basis of a relationship forms a connection. It provides the idea that reciprocating energy creates a bond and cycling energetic flow. Working relationships with spirits and divinity are often established in western cultures by observing things in the physical and as external practices or series of devotional rituals.

The practice of communing with spirits and working with the energies of the universe are actually internal and external practices. For most practitioners, it's often understanding or interpreting what is happening internally that requires development. Entities and spirits carry their own moods and motives, especially if they were once human, but it can become confusing when we enter the auric field of spirits and people unintentionally and absorb their information psychically.

The difficulty comes down to recognizing and identifying what energy is produced by you and what energy is produced by another. Have you ever walked into a room and felt immediately angry or uneasy? You may have sensed the energetic impressions left by others, either from this plane or another. Paying attention and becoming aware of these changes in ourselves and the environment is a primary step in learning how to work with these energies.

Not only will you need to learn to pay attention to your senses but also how to enter different states of consciousness. These different states are proven as producing specific waves called alpha and theta waves. The good news is, reaching these states can be simple and achieved through meditation and visualization. We can access higher levels of consciousness through various altered states. These states can be achieved by merging our consciousness and etheric bodies into oneness with the Supreme Consciousness, which is mostly achieved through meditation.

Meditation, more often than not, plays a large part in helping practitioners enter the necessary states for the efficiency of intention and visualization. Some people, however, have developed their skills to access the states without the need for lengthy meditation and can be done in five minutes or less. But just like any skill set or talent, the more you practice, the stronger and better at it you become. The truth is the same if you discontinue practice for any reason, you tend to lose that strength. It can be much more difficult building up the mastery or condition to be great at something rather than losing it. Losing your strength of abilities can happen much more rapidly. The point being, anything worthwhile takes time and practice. Committing to a beginner mindset and being a continuous learner will aid you in your growth and strengthening of your mystical skills. Understand that the work is a school of constant learning, and no matter the mastery of your skill set or talent, be of humility in knowing there is always more to learn and understand. A significant part of facilitating and mastering the work comes down to effective intention and visualization.

The work has a number of parallels and similarities with magic. Despite the fact that psychics are adamant that their talents are not magical, I've discovered a lot of overlap between those with enhanced clair senses and practitioners of magic due to their commonality in interacting with spirits. True magic is the art of causing change in conformity with will. The mechanism of this is dependent on the intent of the individual. Like willpower, magical intent is a process of seeing what you want so clearly that your thoughts, focus, and intention pushes it through the planes of existence to make it happen. It's knowing that you have a vision powerful enough to create a living entity. The universe has no other option but to rearrange its conditions to accommodate the event—it can no longer post-pone the inevitable because it has already been manifested. As I mentioned before, at the core of this power is love. It's love that makes our thoughts reality and assists in opening the connection to spirits. Remember your reasons for wanting to connect with spirits and realize that the most powerful connections come from love.

Part of communicating with spirits is strengthening your relationship with them, which comes down to how your beliefs support your interpretation of energetic relationships. Like I mentioned before, spirit work is a very individual practice, and what works for some will not work for others. You will need to establish a foundation of your own beliefs to support your alignment. One of the greatest blocks to the work is fear, so be assured that the practices and theories mentioned here are safe. In the words of Lon Milo DuQuette, author and magician, "The most important secret of magic and of life is: do not be afraid!"[4]

Fear is at the root of limiting our connection to invisible energies. On some level, everyone and everything is already connected. The control over the level of connection to energy acts like a floodgate. If you close the gate, the connection is severed and the flow of energy becomes blocked and weak. When you open the gate, the connection flows through strongly. People are often closed off due to many variables of fear, including societal programming, limiting beliefs, traumas, unhealthy habits, negative thought patterns, a disconnect from natural elements, and a limited connection to life force. Those blockages can be immense or minor, making for strong or weak flows of energy.

Energy workers and psychics often have a genetic or environmental predisposition (some say a talent) to interact with and open the flow of energy more readily, but ultimately they are all just people who have developed control over these floodgates and understand how to control the opening and closing of these doors. It can become easy for anyone to get overwhelmed if they don't know how to control the lever to these floodgates.

---

4. DuQuette, Lon Milo, *Low Magick: It's All in Your Head, You Just Have No Idea How Big Your Head Is* (Woodbury, MN: Llewellyn Publications, 2010), 5.

Chapter 2

DEVELOPMENT AND ATTUNING

It's incredibly important when you begin to attune yourself to invisible energies, you must be gentle with yourself. Forcefulness will only cause damage, and walking the spiritual path must be a lifelong commitment. Don't rush yourself if you aren't immediately seeing the results you hoped for. Force and frustration, just like fear, will only lead to blockages, low vibrations, and channeling negative entities. Don't be afraid of intuitive development, but instead proceed with care. Everyone is capable of intuitive development to work with energies. Everyone experiences intuitive messages consciously or unconsciously; the trick is to start paying attention. If you're having trouble differentiating between logic, imagination, or intuition, try practicing intuitive analysis.

Intuition is a mixture of understanding your instincts combined with receptive information from the senses. When you follow this kind of information or messages that your body tells you is true and you trust it, you gain an inner sense of knowing. This knowledge, combined with an activated third eye, is what practitioners utilize to hear and communicate with spirits. Psychics and mediums use it for channeling; magicians and witches use it in magic. It's a very practical skill to implement with energy and spirit work.

Furthermore, psychic and intuitive development is all a matter of balance. Just as it takes work and dedication to perfect skills or techniques, forcing yourself to become great can also be harmful. Think of a bodybuilder, if she doesn't give herself enough time to recuperate or rest, she could cause her body harm from fatigue, broken-down muscles, and being overworked. She needs to allow for rest and recuperation to give the body time to rebuild and improve. The same is true for energy workers. Remember to practice and dedicate yourself, but don't overdo it. Allow for the flow of energy to occur instead of trying to force it, and you'll see much more positive results.

In order to tune in to unseen energies, practitioners use many different techniques that they've practiced over time, like building a muscle. Their abilities are often developed through forms of meditation or trance work and start off by using exercises that are intended to help prepare the individual for meditation. Centering techniques are designed to take the mind off of the ordinary waking state and into a deep relaxation state. Centering is a much more quick and simple practice and is usually mistaken for meditation. Meditation does not happen until the mind has entered a state of inner stillness or silence, or has experienced emptiness called the void.

You may have heard the term "clear your mind," and in some cases, this phrase can be beneficial. But what we need to actually do is begin with centering, which is a practice of focus and understanding how to be present to strengthen clarity. Although each tradition will carry its own version and definition of what centering is, simply put, centering is to merely direct our focus and either visualize energy so we can begin to utilize it or create the environment required for spiritual communication. This does not indicate that the mind is altogether empty or cleared. In this instance, the goal of the practitioner is to remove distraction and form a foundation for energy work. Centering is a primary step in spirit communication and in the work. It's necessary to create a space for clear spirit communication and allow a receptive flow of energy. Centering is simple enough, and in this book I'll give step-by-step instructions to achieve it by focusing on the breath in chapter eight.

Once you can experience your environment with all of your senses, you will develop the tools needed for spirit work. Some practices relate centering to mindfulness, in which you focus on being intensely aware of what you're sensing and feeling in the moment, without interpretation or judgment. Practicing mindfulness can involve breathing methods, visualizations, and other practices to relax the body and mind. For some, they can easily shut out our busy world; for others it will be challenging to slow down and notice things—for them, practice is vital.

Before you are ready to practice things like intuitive analysis, centering, or meditation, keep in mind that thoughts will enter. Allow for the flow of thoughts to come and go. Do not hang on to them but instead notice them and allow them to leave your mind's eye. This encourages the flow of energy and strengthens the practice of embracing meditative states instead of combating whatever comes into your mind. This is why meditation can be difficult for many—they try too hard to silence and clear all the chatter of the mind, when really all we want to do is be in the present. Understanding that thoughts come and go will allow for a flow of energy so that we can decipher what is of our internal consciousness and what is coming from external sources.

PRACTICING INTUITIVE ANALYSIS EXERCISE

Whenever you have a choice to make, find a place where you feel comfortable and removed from distraction. Appreciate and focus on the beauty around you. This can be literal beauty in nature, such as the reflection of the sun on water, or the beauty you see in your environment. I once saw beauty in the structure of my bookshelf being categorized and orderly. Once you focus on your appreciation for your environmental beauty and focus on your breathing, ask yourself, *What option will align me with my highest purpose or what decision is best for me?* Don't search for the answer, instead, wait and listen for words, phrases, or images that come into your mind and take note. There may be a flood of information or just a trickle, but notice which one feels truer and more aligned to your heart.

Place your logical mind aside and lean into the option that just feels absolute. If you can, learn to listen to that feeling of knowing it's the right choice. In life, you are often presented with guidance in forms of whispers, signs, and synchronicities for the best-case scenario and outcome. Your first instinct is usually correct. Allow yourself to trust your instincts and what your body tells you instead of listening to the thoughts of your mind. Pondering choices with your mind is the opposite of what we're doing. Listen to how you feel, regardless of if you understand it. This is the beginning of learning to trust your intuition, by how you feel rather than what you think.

Chapter 3

THE IMPORTANCE OF CONSENT

Developing intuition and connecting with your higher self is critical in spirit work because there are many ways in which spirits use to communicate. In Western traditions and culture, we're often taught to administer logic and science to prove scenarios. Spirituality exists outside of measuring with our minds. The answers can be explained, but not by this way of thinking. Give yourself permission to listen to how you feel, and use all of your other senses instead of leading with the logical mind. In spirit work, the logical mind can limit our connections. We must begin to recondition how we think. If you are already someone who has a developed intuition and can listen to your heart over your head, you are already a step ahead.

Permission and consent are not only important for practitioners in reconditioning what they believe and how they think so they can be open to spiritual relationships, but anytime the intention of making contact with a spirit is sought, we must begin by giving them permission to manifest. Giving permission is simple enough: clearly state your intentions out loud in order to make contact with them. When you give permission, also address them so that you are 100 percent aware of who the spirit is that you're giving consent to. If you don't know who the spirit is, you can make more general statements such as "I wish to contact my spirit guides of the highest love and compassion," or "I wish to speak to my paternal ancestors who love and protect me."

For the next exercise, we'll begin making contact by administering consent for your spirit allies called spirit guides. Spiritual allies are always with us—they are entities that work with us for our benefit. More specifically, spirit guides are among these allies and are the best to begin with because they are benevolent, nonphysical entities who have our best interests at heart. They are sanctioned to help us to achieve our true will. They are assigned by your higher self before birth and are invested to assist you on your life's journey and development. The length of time that your spirit guides spend with you may differ. They may be with you your entire life, or just a short period of time, like helping you through a particular moment or with a life lesson.

I like to think of them as an invisible team of life coaches, mentors, and counselors. For this reason, it's best to begin spirit work and develop your intuitive or psychic senses by tuning in with your spirit guides because they are safe and loving spirits.

ADMINISTERING CONSENT EXERCISE

Find a comfortable space without any distractions. If you have access to a speaker, play 963 Hz Solfeggio frequency. 963 Hz sounds can be found on YouTube and popular music streaming channels. Simply choose one to your liking and play it while you perform this exercise. This frequency is associated with awakening intuition and activating the pineal gland. It awakens our crown chakra (Sahasrara) and raises the positive energy and vibrations so we can better connect and establish permission. Listen to this frequency as you meditate.

Visualize a bright light, as bright as the sun radiating love and protection above you. Don't worry if your visualization skills are not perfect; imagining this light is enough to be effective. Visualize the light emanating and flowing down through the top of your head through your crown chakra. Allow it to rest in your heart space and surround you in protective energy. Once you are ready, with your eyes closed and you feel a state of calmness and clarity, mentally or verbally call out to your spirit guides:

"I wish to connect with and open communication with my spirit guides of the highest truth and compassion."

"Spirit guides, I ask you to manifest yourselves to me."

"I am ready to receive your guidance."

"I want to have a relationship with you."

"I allow you to become a part of my life."

"I am grateful for your love, for your guidance, and for the clarity you provide me with."

As you speak these words of power, keep your eyes closed and allow for visions to enter your mind. You may see images or sounds come closer to you in your mind's eye. Just allow thoughts to come and go. Recognize and notice any thoughts that might enter your mind, but do not follow them. Simply focus on your breath and let them pass. As you remain in this receptive state, pay attention to any images, conversations, words, or sounds that occur. You may hear things in your own voice or from someone unrecognizable; witness them without force. Pay attention to your senses. What do you hear? What do you notice? There may be messages provided to you.

This may take one try or several tries before you receive confirmation from your guides. It doesn't matter so much if you have a particularly strong bond or relationship with your spirit guides at that time. Your connection will grow stronger as you build your relationship with them and open up more to receive their messages. The key here is that you practice administering this consent and state your intentions. Allowing spirit allies to be a part of your life is achieved through communicating permission.

Essentially, by setting intentions through consent you are establishing a spiritual contract, or rather establishing boundaries, to allow them to manifest and come to your aid in exchange for a relationship with you. These boundaries are fixed, and I have never required spiritual protection when my intentions are working for my highest good and the highest good of others. Be assured this is a safe practice.

Chapter 4

LIGHT AND DARK

There are a lot of unfounded fears and beliefs spread about spirit work and whether or not it's "evil." The concept of evil is a human construct. We are part of a world of both positive and negative entities, energies, and events. Unfortunately, some people tend to use misinformation to project fear about spirit work. When a powerful organization sells you the idea to fear something, ask why. We must pull back the curtain to discover the root of that fear. Most of the time, once you begin to dive deeper you realize that many fears have been projected onto us with ulterior motives. We think it's to keep us safe, when in actuality it's to govern control and maintain power. Exercise due diligence with research and cross-checking credible resources. I wholeheartedly believe that the information in this book should not be used to control or restrict your beliefs, but to empower you to use critical thinking and discern what you believe to ease any apprehension, doubts, or anxiety toward spiritualism.

Spirit work can absolutely benefit its practitioners. For the determined, brave, and investigative practitioner, this can bring about a greater understanding of universal truths, and when applied appropriately can guarantee measurements of improved health, prosperity, and wisdom. We all have the ability to make a conscious choice of connecting with light or dark energies—both exist simultaneously. Simply put, the work is working with energy, and it is a metaphysical practice that can create change in our physical reality. Its categorizations rely entirely on the practitioner performing it. The work itself is a spiritual and sacred art form. Practitioners can tap into the source of power—a natural energy that is entirely unbiased and neutral to objectives—and then use it as intended. So, when the discussion of the work centers around being good or evil, it is neither until a practitioner utilizes this natural force. So, what becomes the label is the intention of the practitioner—creative or destructive purposes, help or harm, and not the work or energies themselves.

This idea that they must be separate and categorized as good or evil is again a human construct, and this perception is relative to societal and individual beliefs. We use many metaphors to categorize the meaning of things like demon or angel. Energies are not only black and white; this categorization warps the understanding of energy and spiritualism. To truly understand an energy's nature, it cannot be categorized as easily as saying it is only of the light or dark, good or evil, high or low. It is neither, because it is both, existing as one. Energy has both positive and negative charges, likewise in energetic terms, spirits, entities, beings, angels, and demons are both.

Therefore, the work has nothing to do with evil, and most practitioners don't even work with the idea of evil at all. Anyone with an interest in working with darker spirits should already understand that the work cannot be categorized or labeled as such. Varied forms of the work, including witchcraft, never actually include such energies or destructive forces. Although some practitioners may choose to work with demons, who's to say the intention of their work is "evil"? Only the practitioner knows that, and even though some practitioners may choose to work with these forces in their practice, fears often arise of something that is misunderstood.

The work is inherently a spiritual practice, and, in actual fact, spiritualism was never categorized or associated with being "evil" until the emergence of modern media and the dawn of new inventions, including the radio and television. Before these inventions, spiritualism was viewed as a very positive practice. Mediumship, channeling messages, and communicating with spirits up until then was about relaying messages of hope and providing closure for peace and love. However, the narrative about spirits was quickly altered with the dawn of these new inventions as a form of entertainment. Some people enjoy being scared and the adrenaline rush that comes with it. But for the gullible and weak-minded, understanding the difference between fact and fiction became skewed due to the popularity and rise of entertainment.

Every energy you work with, whether it's a spirit, deity, angel, or demon, has both sides—the light and the dark—and your intention is more accurately what receives the categorization of light or dark. Like I mentioned before, you are capable of both light and dark, just as spirits are. It is all a matter of choice.

We must then understand that a spirit's nature, intent, or motives are not reflective of the literary use of their label. This is evident by what we already discussed to be true about the work—it is neither good nor evil, and it is the intent of its use that specifies its purpose. Intentions alone specify its nature, not the categorization or label. But when we refer to spirits as angels or demons, we're referring to them in literary terms as metaphors. This does not depict their true energetic nature in a practical sense.

In order to be an effective spiritual worker or practitioner, we need to be open to a multitude of meanings or definitions that span all cultures associated with words and language. We must understand the importance of our intention and associations through language and not the word itself. Since all words were made up by humans, the meaning of a word can vary and be redefined to fit a person's beliefs more accurately based on many variables. Categorizing light or dark energy are all befitting of perspective and intention.

My wish for you is to have the freedom to develop your own beliefs and that they are generated for you by you from what you can discerningly understand using your own critical thinking to decipher information and experiences. The truth is, no one can choose your moral compass and ethical code for you. Although most people do abide by universal ethics, what is right or wrong when it comes to your beliefs and perception is often individual. The problem is, popular ideas tend to rule all. What needs to be more widely accepted is individual perception and experience. That is how you will gain the clarity you need to move forward in spirit work. Believing something simply because someone told you it was so will not give you the results you desire, and it will constantly leave you second-guessing your instincts and intuition. However, learning how to use your own discernment and tune in to your own feelings from your personal experiences will make for much more powerful results.

Moreover, entities are not to be constrained to fitting into something so simple as black and white categories, or light and dark—they are more nuanced than that and therefore cannot be described as inherently good or inherently evil. For example, dark deities like Lilith and Lucifer are both feared because of their demonic associations, but they are also found to be venerated for their protective qualities. If you remove their literary context, their energy is both, just how people are capable of portraying both.

Whether it's of the light or of the dark, working with spirits all comes down to your intention behind initiating a relationship, and that is why intent is so important. If a practitioner's goal is to evoke the embodiment of evil, then it will more than likely bring about nothing more than a bit of spiritual anarchy or chaos, and at the very worst, may cause some actual harm. But if the goal is to discover the mysteries of hidden knowledge, defy social structure, or harness and experience healing powers that the spiritual education of darkness can provide, the experience can be a very positive one—even if that entity is referred to as the "Devil."

In fact, the "Devil" from ancient folklore is a construct of very different behaviors and traits from that of the Christian Satan. Practitioners who work with either find it useful to think of them as different entities, and not all demonic practices are satanic. In my research, I've found that most Satanists don't work with demons at all. In fact, the author of *The Satanic Bible*, Anton LeVey, was an atheist. The Church of Satan is an atheist institution that views the existence of the Christian God and Devil as insufficient, mistaken, or outweighed by arguments and evidence indicating there isn't reason to believe in their existence.

Atheistic Satanists have no interest in worshipping the Devil and regard Satan as a symbol better characterized as a representative of the humanistic traits that Christians demonize—like pride, liberalism, and individualism. Satanic magic actually does not involve working with demons, and although Satanists may use a symbol for Satan in ritual, they don't actually worship a divinity. People who work with demons, more than just utilizing symbols in rituals, are rarely practicing satanic magic, and magical workings with demons seldom have anything to do with Satanism, paganism, or religion.

There are some historical records that indicate witches who've worked with demons or the "Devil" for the intent to harm and hurt others—otherwise known as maleficium—but these are more often, if not all, fabricated cases from their accusers during the era of witch hunts in America and Europe. In these cases, the people accused were never involved in working with Satan, performing black masses, devil worship, or any such practices. The only "evil" then were the actions of those who murdered innocent people, whether they were accusers, bystanders, or executioners—taking someone's life and torturing them against their will. Those are the true faces of evil.

Although working with demons is highly uncommon in witchcraft and folk magic, which is most commonly practiced among the middle and lower social classes, it's actually in Goetic and ceremonial magic that records dictate calling and working with demons, which is more commonly practiced by those in high social standings.

Ceremonial magic incorporates a wide variety of long, elaborate, and often complicated rituals. The more prominent practitioners of ceremonial magic include Aleister Crowley and John Dee, and in most cases are synonymous with it. A key element to performing ceremonial magic is the invocation and evocation of entities, both angels and demons, from Jewish and Christian lore.

There are many categories of ceremonial magic, including Enochian and Goetic. Enochian magic comes from the recordings of John Dee and Edward Kelley, who were said to receive their information directly from angels. Goetia is the term for a type of magic that conjures or summons spirits, especially demons. Ceremonial magic is challenging, to say the least, and requires a lot of study because of its complexity. It is demanding and not situated for the beginner practitioner. The goal of Goetic magic is dependent on the practitioner's intent and which demon or entity they summon, and can include anything from curing illness to gaining wealth. These entities' motives and moods can vary from obsequious and dutiful to untamed and defiant. Nevertheless, it would be wise for practitioners to remember the most important rule of conjuration—never summon what you cannot banish!

Stories of people making deals with demons or the Devil at a crossroad commonly exist in folklore and myths, and while crossroads and thresholds are highly active places to meet and interact with entities, the story of the crossroad spirit is much older than Christian belief. Crossroad spirits often go by other names, and, depending on your beliefs, these spirits are not malevolent at all, in fact, they can be fiercely protective and loving toward their devotees. In Greek mythology, crossroads were associated with both Hermes and Hecate. In the Vodou tradition, Papa Legba is the Iwa of crossroads and a messenger to the spirit world. When working with spirits, it's important to identify who you are working with and not just allow for labels or other's beliefs to dictate who that entity is.

In my experience, it's much easier to form a relationship with a deity or spirit with personified traits rather than an abstract divine force. Aside from spiritually fulfilling relationships, entities in any context can be powerful allies. But very few of these entities are 100 percent good or 100 percent bad. Just like people, deities have strengths and weaknesses. Even the Abrahamic God has flaws, and if you don't believe me, you may need to revisit the Old Testament. The point of it is, you know how to assess the risks associated with certain individuals, so apply the same amount of discernment you would use for human relationships as you would for the spiritual kind.

A category of spirits that requires more discernment is demons. The concept of demons is much older than what most people relate them to.

Demons are often associated as dark or malevolent forces and entities, but after my research I regard them as often rebellious and independent, although intensely powerful beings. Popular belief depicts them to associations with Abrahamic religions, but mention of them dates back much further to ancient religions and philosophy. Therefore, beliefs associated with demons and the concept of working with them does not classify a practitioner as working with Abrahamism and Semitic religions.

Even the etymology of the word *demon* depicts inaccuracies with its beliefs of being evil. The word *demon* originates from the Ancient Greek word "daimon." Its meaning is defined as a lesser god or divine power. In this sense they serve as a protector, guardian, or patron spirit. Their association with malevolence didn't appear until the rise of Christianity and was used in a Latin version of the Bible authorized and used by the Roman Catholic Church. It was with the spread of Abrahamism and Semitic religions where Western cultures adopted its definitions as unclean spirits and associated with heathens.[5]

As you can see, the literary sense of the word is very different from the true nature of a spirit. In religious context, the majority of modern Western society associates the word demon with that of something evil, especially in Christianity. However, in psychology, the daimonic refers to a natural human impulse to affirm, assert, perpetuate, and increase the self to its complete totality.

Another example of the nature of a spirit versus its literary metaphor appears in the book series *His Dark Materials* by Phillip Pullman, the author uses the Latin spelling *dæmon* as a being that takes form as an animal, like the outer physical manifestation of a person's inner self. Along with the spelling, Pullman refers to the originating word from the Latin noun, describing it as an aspect of the human nature of his characters and not associated with evilness. He develops a character's dæmon entirely as its own character, connected to their counterparts and in relation to a conscience and internal voice, similarly to the role of the character Jiminy Cricket in

---

5. Harper, Douglas, "Etymology of demon," Online Etymology Dictionary, accessed November 19, 2021, https://www.etymonline.com/word/demon.

Disney's *Pinocchio*. Within the series by Pullman, the "dæmons" appear in the opposite gender, establishing a balance of a character's true nature—like an outward and visible representation of a balance between the yin and yang, or divine feminine and masculine energies.

The concept of duality and unity of paradoxes is central to the yin-yang philosophy. It suggests that the universe is designed to have balance. Everything is, in fact, both yin and yang. Both sides can exhibit dominant characteristics in their own unique ways. It is important to seek the light within the dark and to recognize the darkness within the light. This idea is at the heart of Tao and is a dynamic construct. It is not static and is constantly blending and balancing. For us to become truly whole, we must embrace both the dark and the light.[6]

Far too often we try to neatly package and label things. My example of how the majority of Western civilizations relate the word *demon* to its contemporary and religious context, rather than the historical meaning or nature of the being, is to demonstrate that beliefs are skewed by language. But imagine now that a demon is capable of both creation and destruction, harm and help. So if a demon is capable of much more than malice, why can't angels be capable of more than mere good?

Another example to look at is high and low magic. To the naive and uneducated, they may think high magic may depict a holy practice and low magic an infernal one. But just as I've discussed before, intent is far more depictive of a practice or the nature of an energy. In truth, high and low magic can be simply categorized as such: low magic is nature-based or earthly, and high magic is ceremonial or ritualistic. In this instance, high and low magic simply differ in application and appeal to different personalities and tastes.

Although high magic often includes working with spirits and is associated with the other world, it is said to not be used for bringing about earthly pleasures and physical manifestations. High magic's purpose is to gather

---

6. Abel, C., "The Duality, Paradox, and Harmony behind the YinYang," Medium, accessed May 20, 2020, https://medium.com/the-philosophers-stone/symbology-of-symbols-the-yinyang-7da94af198a6.

knowledge, and it is centered on a "initiation" that symbolises a union or change from being primarily unconscious to mostly conscious.[7] Low magic is linked to the word's etymology in that it is associated with this world rather than the heavens. These types of magic are neither good nor evil; they are neutral until a practitioner attaches intent to them.

For example, think of a pencil. A pencil can be used as a tool for beneficial purposes or harmful purposes; the intent relies on the person wielding the tool. The same rings true for the work. Remember, the moon reflects the light of the sun as it makes its way across the night's darkness. As the sun illuminates all things, it also casts shadows on what it touches. Regardless, whether or not you are intending to connect with spirits does not depict that you are necessarily performing high or low magic. The point is, there is good in every evil and evil in every good. Although there is darkness within light and light contained in darkness, we do not try to understand it; it simply is a matter of fact. Everything that is related to a function or position has its own intrinsic value.

In short, it's up to you to decide how information aligns with your beliefs. Should your practice include working with light or dark, angels or demons? It comes down to your intent—do you mean help or harm? Are you working for a person's greatest good, or seeking to have control over them? How you perform the work is all a matter of choice. Nevertheless, we cannot deny the existence of both light and dark.

---

7. Weschcke, Carl L, "The Goal of High Magick is Initiation," Llewellyn Worldwide, accessed Feb 12, 2020, https://www.llewellyn.com/encyclopedia/article/25576.

Chapter 5

THE TYPES OF ENTITIES YOU MAY ENCOUNTER

There are many kinds of spirits that practitioners may encounter. Although this is not an exhaustive list, these categories will help you differentiate their energies and decide if it is something you want to connect with to form a working relationship. It's valuable and important to have an understanding of the different types of energies before working with them so you know what you may be dealing with and therefore can correctly identify the kind of energy you would like to work with in your practice.

Land spirits: As the name implies, these are spirits who dwell within particular places or features of the land. They are connected to natural places or things, such as a certain river or a specific mountain. There are a multitude of these kinds of spirits, and some have achieved deity or godlike status. For example, the Hindu goddess Ganga is the goddess of the Ganges River. To begin working with land spirits, it's important to identify sacred places in your area. These can be places like springs, crossroads, peaks, shores, and other thresholds. Next, spend time in these places and get familiar with their energy. If you are going to leave offerings, it's important to leave ones that are environmentally friendly, or even better, to clean a site of any litter.

Proper practice of working with land spirits includes asking them for permission to enter their domain. Simply wait until you sense that it is okay to proceed. Address them respectfully, introduce yourself, and just listen. It's important to pay attention to what rituals and offerings you intend to leave or create, be conscious of the land and that you aren't leaving anything harmful. You can always communicate with your land spirits and ask for guidance if you need clarity on offerings, but clean water is quite commonly accepted.

Spirits of place: When a spirit has imprinted or is associated with a location like a town or specific building, it can be a powerful place to meet them. The history of these spirits being venerated and revered spans worldwide. For example, household spirits are found in many cultures like the Scandinavian *Tomte*, also referred to as *Nisse*. In English and Scottish folklore, a small, industrious spirit that inhabits houses and barns is called a brownie. The *húsvættir* originates from Nordic culture and is a collective term for keepers of the household. To build a relationship with household spirits, begin by acknowledging and greeting them. Connecting with them can make for a peaceful and positive home environment. If you wish to leave an offering, simply leave out a small portion of cream or milk and keep the area comfortable and tidy. Clean water can also be used for an offering.

Animal spirits: Animal spirits can refer to the archetype of an animal species or a singular animal spirit that manifests. Generally, they are benevolent spirits, which makes them much easier for beginners to work with. For example, *fylgjur* or the *fylgja* appear in Norse mythology as an animal attendant spirit and remain closely connected to the persona of its owner. Familiars are spirits that take the form of animals who aid witches and cunning folk with their magical practice. Shamanic traditions include animal guides as protector spirits—a person's power animal can be met through meditation and rituals like journeying or vision quests. The animal a person connects with is often unexpected. If you are lucky enough to have met your power animal, research the characteristics and qualities to further understand the meanings and messages—the experience and discoveries can be incredibly fulfilling.

If you feel compelled, you may wish to honor your local animal spirits. Some practitioners place items connecting to the animal on their altar. Feathers are an example of offerings for those who connect with birds. Offerings will differ; pay attention to the characteristics of the animal spirit guide to determine what would be appropriate. Clean water is also acceptable. A good rule of thumb is to ask for permission from the local spirits before taking anything in nature and intuitively wait for confirmation. It's considered polite to leave an offering in return. The offering does not need to be necessarily physical. The act of reducing your carbon footprint can be considered an offering.

Elementals: Elementals, also referred to as nature spirits, are the life energy that runs through all living things and the elements of earth, air, water, and fire. Other traditions may include additional elements. These spirits are identified by a special association with some form or function within the earth's natural surroundings. Nature spirits or elementals don't have a one-size-fits-all explanation. Many Aboriginal cultures have beliefs of spirits that pervade all of existence and can be found in the land, water, air, and fire, as well as in all living things. In some traditions there are crossovers between land spirits and elementals; however, elementals tend to be more primeval and are not sanctioned to a specific location.

Spirits such as gnomes, fairies, leprechauns, and elves are all closely linked to the earth element. Earth spirits combine the elements for practical and grounded ways, working with consciousness.

Air spirits, known as sylphs, can manipulate weather. They are present in the sky and are undetectable to the naked eye. A sylph can detect even the tiniest changes in wind, humidity, temperature, or air pressure. The air element is represented through dancing, singing, performance, and artistic expression. It elicits positive emotions such as joy, contentment, amusement, and happiness. It serves as a reminder of the joy and beauty that may be found in life. Art and music can freely flow into our life because of the quality of the air we breathe.[8]

Nixies, naiads, ondines, undines, mermaids, and water nymphs are all names for water spirits. They are the embodiment of water's fluidity, nurturing, relaxing, releasing, receptivity, and beauty in nature. Although they are commonly shown as half human, half fish, they can take on any shape.

Salamanders are associated with the element of fire. They are concerned with the intersection of passion, power, and knowledge. Salamanders also deal with motivating factors and a person's inner will, in the same way that fire is broad and active. If an individual has suppressed anger, the fire element can cause fury and a drive to control, as well as paranoia when one's safety is endangered.

Once attuned to the elemental energy, practitioners can often hear spirits through the earth, bodies of water, fire, and in the wind. Adopting an animistic belief system, viewing the world from a nonhuman point of view and ascribing life to everything, can assist in connecting with these spirits.

Fairies: Fairies are beings who are strongly connected to the earth plane. Fairies generally serve and nurture the earth, including the plant and animal kingdoms. Ancient folklore depicts that fairies were once much more present and visible by humans but hid themselves as humanity fell into greed and destruction and forgot their connection with the natural world. In folklore, fairies are described as spirits with humanlike attributes, have magical abilities, and the power to shape-shift. They are depicted as having an inclination or natural tendency for tricks and mischief, although some praise their kindness and generosity. With a fairy, essentially the energy you put out is what you will receive. It is also believed that fairies cannot

---

8. Colosimo, Natalie, "Elementals and Earth Spirits," The Psychic School, accessed Oct 20, 2021, https://psychicschool.com/elementals-and-earth-spirits.

tell lies, which makes them experts in deception or ambiguity.

If you want to have a relationship with fairies, you must have your wits about you. Working with fairies should be approached carefully. A number of rules must be followed in order to remain in their good graces. To keep out of trouble, never purposely disrespect them and always be courteous. Many people have the belief that it is impolite to say "thank you" or "I'm sorry" to fairies. The reason is that it diminishes their act of kindness. It would be wiser and a better way to express your gratitude by stating something more along the lines of "I express my gratitude or appreciation for…" or "You are most kind," and an apology can be made by simply saying, "My apologies," "Pardon me," or "I express regret."[9] Offerings include things like honey and sweet, shiny, or natural gifts. Also, reducing your carbon footprint and making an effort to help the environment are regarded as positive acts to them.

Ancestral spirits: Ancestor spirits are human relatives that have passed on. They may be of biological relations, or those who had other connections to you—like having been part of a community or generalized guardian spirits of a family. Paying tribute or veneration to ancestral spirits is a great way to begin spirit work because there's usually already a bond or connection established with your ancestors. Because of their love and protection toward you, they will generally want to come to your aid. Keep in mind, challenges can be presented in spirit work with ancestors if the practitioner doesn't know their lineage, their history, or if they don't feel particularly close with them. If you want to work with your ancestral spirits, the best place to start is to trace your family roots and research their history. Some practitioners create altars to honor them and to use in their sacred space for their work. Items, food, or drink that an ancestor was once fond of is placed upon the altar. If you're curious about altars and their use, you can find information on them in chapter 11.

---

9. "A Hitchhiker's Guide to Faerie," Faeriepedia, accessed Jun 12, 2020, https://faeriepedia.weebly.com/a-hitchhikers-guide-to-faerie.html.

Angels: Most people nowadays refer to angels with the widespread ideas and concepts from Christian belief—that they are winged humanlike beings who are the messengers of God. Islamic angels, or *malaikah*, are believed to be created before humans and communicate the messages from Allah. Regardless of religious beliefs, angels are incredibly powerful, divine spirits. There is some debate about the nature of true angels because of their association with spirit guides. A guardian angel is another name for spirits who are most commonly associated with spirit guides because of their loving disposition. It's believed that they are more supportive spirits for beginners to start working with, whether you are religious or not.

However, angels do not have a preference about where you draw your faith and beliefs from. According to John Dee and Edward Kelley's Enochian Magic system, there are several hierarchies of angels, or intelligent rulers, set over such things as the planets, the stars, and the four quarters of the earth. *The Arbatel*, an original sourcebook of angel magic, recognizes the existence of biblical angels, but also implies the existence of the pagan gods, entities that were subjugated to the Judeo-Christian God, thus being rephrased as angels and demons. These angelic entities are capable of both creation and destruction. The pre-Christian magi angels' appearance resembles much more something of a nightmare than the ethereal winged human-esque beings, which some people prefer to think of. Specificity is key if you wish to work with angels; they are divine beings of great power. Research is essential to make sure you know exactly who or what you are contacting and working with. Offerings made to angels are most commonly not tangible; they are usually energetic. Summoning and invoking them is lengthy and complicated, and not for the beginner.

Demons: Demons are entities that are typically associated with evilness and malevolent behaviors or characteristics. Western culture often characterizes demons from Christian beliefs or other Semitic religions, but demons are also found throughout other religions such as Hinduism and Judaism. Demons aren't entirely different from angels—neither demons nor angels have ever been human, so they don't understand or relate to what it is to be human. It is of no concern to them to make your path easier, and both can be destructive in their nature to bring you what you want. Throughout historical myths and religious documentation, demons are considered to be opposers and masters of defiance. The truth is, demons have their own agenda. Working with them can be very ambiguous and not for beginners. If you should be lucky enough to understand a demon's motives and align them for your own benefit, or learn how to control them, they can make for very powerful allies. There are several ways to banish them, including sulfur and blessed water. Calling on angels and deities can also be performed for protection. Most commonly, workings with demons are found in Goetia. For Solomonic magicians, demons can make great employees; however, for those who aren't adept at such workings, they can be the worst bosses.

Deities: In polytheistic religions, deities are worshipped as gods or goddesses. In monotheistic religions, like Christianity, they are considered the supreme being, creator, and authority of faith. Simply put, deities are divine or sacred spirits. They are incredibly powerful and vary amongst different cultures, each with their own myths, traits, and morality.

Working with them can be a very rewarding experience and an opportunity to acknowledge the divine in a personified manner with human characteristics. For anyone who would like to develop a relationship and work with deities, I recommend starting by researching what interests you. Are you drawn to ancient Greek myths? Or do you want to learn about Egyptian gods and goddesses? Choose what you feel compelled to study and learn about and then use that knowledge as the foundation to build your practice.

Within your studies, you'll find what offerings are acceptable for certain deities. Clean and fresh water is almost universally accepted. I've found it beneficial to charge the water with ruling planetary alignment that is associated with a patron. For instance, Athena's ruling planet is the moon, so water charged under the light of the moon is a perfectly acceptable offering. Although each relationship will vary, one common denominator to remain in their good graces is to treat deities with the utmost respect.

A lot of devotees will try to dive right into deity work; however, many don't understand the long journey and commitment that it takes to form a relationship. If working with deities interests you, first try forming relationships with your ancestors and local land spirits. This is a great way to build a foundation and realize that their existence is in connection to and with regard to other spirits.

Cosmic beings: Cosmic beings, also known as extraterrestrials, star beings, and extra-dimensional beings, are from other planets and often exist in a different dimension. It's believed that some are so far advanced that they can travel across dimensions, time, and space. There are many different kinds of species and levels to their existence. In New Age beliefs, Starseeds, or star people, are believed to be traveling souls with cosmic-being lineage who incarnated on Earth to inspire and heal humankind. The ideas and concepts around Starseeds and these beings come to us through channelers. Just as the species of cosmic beings vary, so do their motives and intent. Some incarnate to help humans evolve, and some seek to support a darker mission. It's important to note that not every one of these souls intends love and light. However, one indicator that you may be a Starseed is a feeling of longing for home and having a sense like Earth is not where you originated from—you might feel like the human experience is foreign.[10]

10. Wagner, Paul, "Are You A Starseed? Read These 27 Starseed Characteristics," Gaia, accessed Nov 15, 2020, https://www.gaia.com/article/am-i-a-starseed-types-characteristics.

Chapter 6

FOUNDATIONS OF A GOOD PRACTICE

Developing and maintaining relationships with spirits can be extremely beneficial to practitioners. Remembering these criteria will assist you in developing correct etiquette and a foundation for your practice in order to stay in the good graces of spirits. This information is very useful for establishing and maintaining a positive practice.

Study: Research is critical in spirit work since it is typically the beginning of a relationship with a spirit. In order to create a relationship with a spirit, you must first fully comprehend them. When you discover more about a spirit, you strengthen your bond with them, which is essential if you wish to work together. Because the etiquette for engaging with different spirits differs, it's vital to recognize who or what you're dealing with. Deities, for example, have distinct requirements for devotees, and those standards sometimes vary for each pantheon. If you choose to connect with your ancestors, how you communicate and act with them is dependent on who they were in life—their character, culture, and beliefs. This is why it's important to know beforehand who it is you are connecting with.

Learning who you're connecting with is simple, especially with deities. For most who venture into spirit work, they feel compelled to research what interests them or what attracts them, like a particular pantheon, or a certain god or goddess. Because there's a plethora of information available, it's easy to research their history and myths.

Lesser-known spirits like land spirits and spirits of place can be more challenging to find information on, but there are some things you can do to help. For instance, acknowledge the kind of spirit you are interacting with, i.e., ancestral spirit, land spirit, et cetera. Next, look for examples of what a particular spirit is usually like and how they are characterized. Lastly, consider how your discoveries apply to the spirit you want to interact with.

If you want to connect with your home spirits, for example, looking at how different cultures engage and connect with them is a good place to start. You may notice that they occasionally make food or drink offerings. Discovering more about your local environment's flora and wildlife can also help in learning more about a spirit. Did the spirit live in a tree before coming to you? What were their origins and what shape would they take? Would it be small, nimble, and humanoid, or would it resemble a typical house spider? Answering these questions can help you have a better idea of how to go forward and develop a bond with spirits.

Be considerate: Being respectful of spirits means more than just being polite. Although proper etiquette is very important when interacting and forming a relationship with a spirit, the way in which you display that etiquette is largely based on who you are interacting with. Good manners differ depending on culture or history, and what it is to be polite with one spirit may be different with another. Not every spirit wants a lengthy or thorough ritual with tools and chants, but it is important to keep in mind that any interactions with them should be met with thoughtfulness and appropriate consideration. Even in banishing a spirit, respect goes a long way.

These are powerful entities and need to be treated as such. Good manners will have an effect on your desired results and help you to avoid any negative consequences. Generally, good manners include things like civility and leaving offerings. Once your interaction is complete, expressing gratitude is also considered polite; however, be attentive to who the spirit is, because, according to fairy lore, saying thank you is a no-no, and there are better ways to express your gratitude. It's possible that a spirit will not connect with you, or that you will not want to work with a spirit for many reasons. Don't try to push it. It's important to be courteous in order to maintain good standing. Look at it as an opportunity, whether a spirit dismisses you or you refuse to work with them—a spirit doesn't want to waste your time, and you shouldn't feel forced to create a connection. If you feel obliged to leave an offering, respect their intentions, or respectfully decline with your reasons, express appreciation clearly and confidently, and move on.

Reciprocate: A partnership, like any successful human relationship, needs a balance of give and take. A mutually beneficial relationship is required to properly interact with spirits—a spiritual ally is not supposed to be a one-sided service. Spirits will not simply perform what you request without expecting anything in return. Similarly, if you put in the effort to develop a relationship and honor it, you will be rewarded.

Offerings should not be considered payment for what you want; it's a bit more complicated than that. But the importance of offerings is that they grant more power to a spirit, and preferred or better offerings can persuade a spirit's willingness to assist you or build a stronger relationship with you. Generally, an offering should be made upon meeting a spirit as a polite introduction. Before asking for anything in return, it's also traditional to make an offering. Offerings, on the other hand, should not be made just for the purpose of receiving something in return. Imagine if a friend attempted to obligate you to perform favors and demanded something in return every time you did something for them. You may begin to doubt their motives and feel used, knowing that their goal is to obtain something from you. It's preferable to avoid this type of agenda by making offerings regularly.

Offerings may not necessarily have to be substantial or tangible. A prayer, a poem, or loving energy, can all be offerings if you intend them to be. Be creative and think of or research what kind of things your spirit ally would like. Consider when a friend's birthday is approaching, you may purchase a present or bake a cake for them. The same can be said about spirits: some enjoy complex and expensive items, while others appreciate the thought and care that goes into them. It's crucial to get to know them so you can figure out what kinds of gifts they enjoy and what they're capable of providing in return. You wouldn't necessarily petition a war goddess for a more loving partner. Specificity is important.

Partner: Spirits should be treated with mutual kindness and respect, much like you would in a relationship—a healthy partnership requires time, care, and effort. Spirit work takes time and dedication, so if that sounds like too much work for you, keep in mind that not everyone is required to participate in the work. It's fine if you accept that it will take a lot more energy and time than you'd like to devote to your practice. If you'd prefer to wait because of the needed commitment, it doesn't mean you're not capable of manifesting on your own.

However, if spirit work appeals to you and seems like something you'd like to explore, the final factor to remember is to regard your connection with your spirit ally as a joint effort. They are not compelled to serve and answer to you. Demanding a spirit for something is the improper method to approach spirit work. Spirits are powerful entities, and they owe you nothing. They are under no obligation to like you, collaborate with you, or even acknowledge you. It's fine if you come across spirits who aren't suited for your work or who aren't right for you. Spirit work, in its essence, is really about being authentic and connecting with and creating genuine bonds with spirits. It's also about assembling a supporting and cooperative group of entities for allies. We get to choose which spirits we wish to associate with, and like any good relationship, it should be a pleasant partnership.[11]

---

11. Sam, "Working with Spirits (Baby Witch Bootcamp Ch. 17)," The Illuminated Witch, accessed May 26, 2021, https://theilluminatedwitch.wordpress.com/2020/07/28/working-with-spirits-baby-witch-bootcamp-ch-17/.

Chapter 7

SPIRITUAL PROTECTION

The truth is, spirits want to form relationships with us just as much as we do them, and most spirits prefer to help us rather than harm us. In fact, spirits cannot do much harm unless we give them permission to and give up the control over ourselves. Spirits are more likely to inspire our talents, provide protection, help us attain clarity, and give us guidance for our higher purpose. They can do a multitude of things that benefit us, and, most times, without us even knowing, are already helping in one way or another.[12]

Author Raymond Buckland states that "like attracts like," and in the case of spirit work, your intentions—whether they're meant for positive or negative outcomes, energies, and events—will connect with and produce as such. Spiritual protection or safeguarding has many uses, but what's often desired is to stop any negative entities from latching on to you. The thing is, if you aren't actively seeking to get in touch with negative energy for your intended outcomes, or coming from a place of fear when working with spirits, the chances of being affected negatively by them are slim. It's important to ask yourself and clearly indicate why you are choosing to communicate and work with spirits. If our intentions aren't baneful or

---

12. Andrews, Ted, *How To Meet and Work With Spirit Guides,* 2nd ed. (Woodbury, MN: Llewellyn Publications, 2006), 23.

seeking assistance from those entities that are, spiritual protection really offers assurance, trust in the work, and precautionary buffers.[13]

The only time I ever felt the need to protect myself was when I was very naive and new to spirit work. Later I realized that my boundaries and intentions are often enough to protect me and the idea of spiritual protection is often exaggerated by unknowledgeable or fear-driven egos. Unless you are someone who is purposefully trying to cause mal-intent or harm, you are spiritually protected. When I use spiritual protection, it's generally for peace of mind and occasionally safeguarding because my objectives, motives, and intentions are pure and good.

I've often heard many beginners parrot information and caution others about the importance of protecting yourself without explaining or understanding spiritual protection themselves. Some new practitioners think that they are being protected by stating they only connect or work with light and love. However, there is more to protection than just speaking it, and it comes down to what's in your heart.

Protection is often brought up in the subject of spirit work because of fear, ignorance, and unfounded ideas generally spread by certain religious groups and belief systems. The truth is, we do not need to fear spirit work. Intentions of working with spirits are most often positive and include things like healing or receiving love and guidance. The work is often aligned with creating change and learning to heal and grow, both internally and externally. Change within brings change without. These changes can be subtle or drastic and can have unexpected effects on the subconscious and reality. Change can be regarded as very positive if intended for desired results and outcomes, but for the beginner or inexperienced practitioner, these changes may not always follow the desirable path. The work may affect you in a way that can cause you to shed any prior aspects of yourself or your perception of your former existence. That it is something to be afraid of only for people who are afraid of change.

Although it's important to safeguard against certain energies, it's only

---

13. Buckland, Raymond, *Buckland's Book of Spirit Communications,* (Woodbury, MN: Llewellyn, 2008), 51.

those who fight against change and don't allow for surrender that can lead to more difficult circumstances. Working with spiritual energy does have the power to alter consciousness and therefore reality. In manifesting our intentions, the necessary changes to align us with the right path can be brought about by destructive forces; we may lose things like friends or a job, and some people have a difficult time accepting their new reality. If what you desire doesn't go as expected, it can result in positive or negative experiences. The question is, Will you embrace those changes, or fight them? If you do the work, change will happen regardless, but if you drag your heels instead of surrendering to them, it can make for a much more difficult process that takes longer.

When it comes to the work, we can really change only ourselves, and once changed, we will then attract our intent. However, in reality, we rarely know exactly what changes we need to make in order to achieve what we desire. That's where spirits can help us. It's something to be mindful of so that we can take the necessary actions to allow for change within so that our intentions can manifest. If you examine and regard change as very positive, then you have nothing to fear. But if you do not, I'm sorry to say you're in for a bumpy ride. Be cautious what you wish for once you've started the work.

Spirits cannot cause you harm as long as you keep authority over your own life. Problems that may arise with spirits are not like in the TV shows and movies. A lot of people enjoy the entertainment that comes with watching a scary show from the safety of their home, but that's what these programs are—entertainment, not fact. Real spirit manifestations do not operate the way entertainment portrays them, and the problems that arise with spirits are nine times out ten instigated by people with poor intentions and questionable ethics—people also may inadvertently give permission to encourage spirits for negative outcomes.

To be clear, possession from malevolent spirits is very rare. It's only when you give up the authority over your own life that you become vulnerable. Keep in mind that, despite its sometimes-negative connotations, "possession" does not have to be a bad thing. A medium may intentionally enable a spirit to utilize his or her voice, hand and/or arm muscles, or other physical parts; nevertheless, he or she should never relinquish absolute control of the body. It's a voluntary arrangement that can be ended at any time. But only in forms of mediumship like direct speech and automatic writing does the medium's body come into play. Under the right circumstances, there is no risk to the medium, yet it may be prudent to take some preventive precautions.

Possession isn't usually connected with positive experiences. However, a successful invocation is essentially a form of voluntary possession. When you invoke a deity or being, you're not inviting it into your home; instead, you're requesting that spirit to come into you. The ceremony of Drawing Down the Moon is a good example of deity invocation. If you're new to spiritual traditions like ritual and ceremonial magic, most people would urge you to wait until you've studied enough to understand what's going on before summoning divinity. Just apply your discernment before you go asking spirits to take possession of you, even if just temporarily. In mediumship, mediums blend their consciousness with that of Divinity to channel or connect with spirits on the other side. That's why it's recommended to start with your spirit guides and ancestors as you find out how you engage with spirits on a personal level. They are often more forgiving and compassionate. It's critical to start interacting with spirits that may not be as volatile or intimidating.

Unlike what you may see in the movies, you can't become possessed unless you consent to it and apply the correct elements. But this is why healing is so important; you don't want your triggers and traumas to influence the control over your life on the physical or spiritual plane. Operating out of a broken or dark place leaves people vulnerable to spiritual influence. Establishing contact and building relationships with spirits should only supplement you and not act as a substitute.

Although there are many reasons for not wanting to work with or establish a connection with a spirit, you will rarely find spirits that enjoy causing havoc and mischief. Even more rarely will you come across any baneful spirits who wish to cause any actual harm. However, just as there are nasty people in the world, there are also nasty spirits. For example, if a person was particularly miserable in life, they will most likely carry that energy into the afterlife, but these entities are more often than not anything more than an annoyance. The simplest way to remove unwanted spirits is also an effective one: tell them to leave.

If you've tried telling them to leave and you still find yourself constantly dealing with misfortune, not by your own doing, you might be experiencing a spirit's energy. Even though dangerous spirits are rare and uncommon, it's good practice to know how to shield yourself and banish them to clear out your space.

There are many methods of spiritual safeguarding, and shielding is just one of them. It's a way of setting energetic boundaries that states that you do not concede to allow spirits to govern over your actions and life, merely that you maintain that control and you allow only what you ask of them. These safeguards must be adhered to, especially when you have not given permission or consent to anything other than what is asked. Just remember, a lot of these methods are unnecessary if you work for your highest good and the highest good of others. You are powerful, so remember to be confident in your intention. It is crucial when you perform the work because it's like enforcing an energetic contract and establishing boundaries. For those who want a little extra safeguarding for peace of mind, here are some other methods.

CLEANSING

Cleansing is a simple method, and plainly put, cleansing is the first method to implement when you need to get rid of lingering energies and spirits. There are several different ways to cleanse your space, so choose whichever one suits you.

Burning substances and using smoke to cleanse your space is a very old method, and there are many different elements you can burn to get rid of unwanted spirits. Sulfur will clear out just about anything, including beneficial spirit allies. I've even heard of a superstition to not use a lighter when lighting candles because sometimes the lighter fluid can include small amounts of sulfur and will ultimately send a spirit away instead of welcoming it. Whether this is true, I'll leave it to you to look up the chemical ingredients in your lighter fluid. But it's my belief that if a lighter or match does actually contain sulfur, it's such a small amount that dissipates after ignition it won't actually cause a spirit to leave. Remember smell is incredibly important to spirits. Pleasant or sacred smells can invite spirits and help with invocation, and unpleasant smells help with banishing and cleansing. If you do end up using sulfur for cleansing, keep in mind that you may need to invite your spirit team back into your space. In addition to smelling terribly, sulfur can be toxic, so only burn small amounts and ventilate sufficiently with open windows.

Burning incense is another way to cleanse your space and objects. Some examples include incense sticks, coil incense, incense cones, and backflow cones. Palo santo wood sticks have emerged as a popular alternative too. The ethical way of harvesting palo santo is sustainable since no trees are being cut down. Instead, they are harvested once the tree dies naturally. If you're a little more creative and want to create your own cleansing incense, combine dried rosemary, bay leaves, and sage. They're easy to grow yourself or find at a local grocer. Add a bit of frankincense and myrrh resin, which are well-known for their magical properties and are antiseptic. You can bundle the items together like in a smudge stick or put them in a heat-resistant dish to burn.

There is a lot of speculation in the magical community about whether a door or window must be open to allow for the energy to exit. Burning magical substances naturally makes smoke and can set off smoke alarms, so if you believe a spirit needs to exit through them, properly venting your space with open windows and doors helps to keep your space from getting smoky and setting off the alarms.

As I've mentioned before, working with energy in large part has to do with intent and visualization. If your intent is to cleanse your space and you don't clearly state and visualize the energies exiting, you've lost half the battle. An open door or window is important for ventilation, so all that will happen if you burn elements in a well-ventilated house is what *you* believe to happen. Whether you believe opening a door or window aids you for clearing out nasties is entirely up to you and your practice. But whatever you choose to believe is the reason for burning substances; it is your business alone.

Sound can be another very quick way to cleanse your area and surroundings. Making loud noises, like beating items together, might surprise, startle, and agitate spirits into fleeing. Cleansing is successful only if you express your intention to remove unpleasant entities, regardless of the method you choose. Make it clear and certain that you want them to go and that they must leave. Tell them in a courteous manner they aren't welcome; there's no need to be harsh. You don't want to insult them, but make sure you put your foot down and state your intentions plainly and clearly with firmness.

Sometimes you may not have the option of smoking up your house. If this is the case, then you can use a wash or powder for cleansing. The great thing about a wash is that you're killing two birds with one stone. A wash is used to wipe down surfaces and doors and mop floors. Washes are great for cleaning and removing all the filth and gunk both energetically and physically. To make a wash, combine water, salt, lemon juice, rosewater, cider vinegar, lavender essential oil, and rosemary or laurel leaf essential oil. For added effect, I will usually follow this up by sprinkling some salt water on my things and around my space.

A cleansing powder is made by combining dry ingredients and then blending or grinding them together to make a fine powder. To grind the ingredients, you can use a food processor, coffee grinder, or a mortar and pestle. To make the powder, you will need salt, lemon peel, roses, lavender, and bay leaves. Make sure the ingredients have been sufficiently dried so they break apart easily. Combine the ingredients together and grind them until they become a fine powder. Then scatter the powder around your space, leave it for a few minutes, and then vacuum, sweep, or dust it.

Cleansing yourself can be just as important as cleansing your space to remove any unwanted connections to spirits and energy. In most cases, a ritual bath or shower is done right after a cleansing so you don't continue to carry any energetic ties with the spirits you've just gotten rid of. The point of a ritual bath is to purify your energy, and this is done with magical ingredients. For this ritual bath, you will need salt, rosemary, sage, and laurel leaves. You can use herbs or essential oils; I've found they have very similar results. If I use the herbs, I like to put them in a reusable mesh bag for easy cleanup.

If you would rather shower instead of taking a bath, then you can make a scrub and use it in the shower to cleanse yourself. For your scrub, mix together salt, rosewater, lemon juice, lavender, rosemary, and bay laurel leaves. Again, you can use either essential oils or dried, crushed herbs. Once you've combined your ingredients, add your favorite body wash to it, and there you go—you now have a scrub to cleanse any old psychic residue. As you wash with your cleansing scrub, visualize your energetic field being purified as the old psychic energy is washed away.

After you've cleansed your space to remove any spirits and energies that you don't want lingering, it would be wise to set some protective boundaries and barriers so spirits can't return or enter. There are countless ways to protect from unwanted or negative energy. Because you can protect just about anything, including yourself, others, spaces, and objects, I'm not going to mention every little thing in great detail, but I will provide you with some of the methods I use to keep you out of any potential harm. Protective measures against negative energies and entities can be administered with simple daily practices or lengthy in-depth rituals. Psychic protection and the type you use will vary based on what you connect with and what suits your practice.

If you are experiencing any kind of spirits that are taking a toll on your mental health, it is crucial you find experts to help you. In my experience, it's very uncommon to encounter spirits of this magnitude, but for your own well-being, make sure you are paying attention to how you feel. Reach out for help from experts if you need it. Now that I've mentioned how important it is to pay attention to your well-being and exercising your right to ask for help, here are some things that have worked for me in protecting against unwanted spirits.

WARDS

Warding can be especially helpful to protect your space from not just unwanted spirits but all energies, including people and creatures too. You can ward spaces or items. Wards are a versatile form of energetic protection that can allow for a semipermeable barrier so that only intended energies can enter and exit or can close off passageways entirely. I like to create protective wards to shield my home of invaders—the spiritual and insect kind. I once had a problem with small beetles constantly coming into my space—they're more annoying than anything—so I warded my space. Almost instantly my beetle problem stopped.

Wards are very simple to conjure. Be clear with your intention and goal of exactly what you want the ward to do. The only limitation a ward can have is by the imagination of the practitioner creating them. Once you define the intention of your ward, keep it in your mind and focus. Visualize energy radiating from your chakras to power the ward. Gather the energy and imagine where you wish it to protect. I like to visualize this energy in different forms, sometimes as pure white energy, sometimes as a flaming sword. It's really up to you.

Locking and warding passageways and mirrors can be a wise thing to do as well since they can act as portals for entities and energies. This can be as simple as using salt to line passageways, or by more elaborate methods—anointing doors, windows, and mirrors with protective oils, followed up by setting your intent. Salt is a powerful protective ingredient. I like to create protective candles by placing them in a dish of salt and setting them in the four corners of my space. I visualize and intend them to work as a shield, radiating energy that acts as a protective barrier.

IRON

In folklore, there is mention of the use of iron for protection from spirits. Iron fences were commonly used for cemeteries because they were believed to keep the spirits in. It's believed that hanging a horseshoe made of iron above an entranceway will keep evil spirits from entering. You can also protect a space by placing iron in the four corners of your home.

PLANTS

Some practitioners and herbalists will attest to plants being very protective. Magical ingredients like rosemary and sage are commonly used in protective spellcraft. Aloe is also said to be highly protective, not to mention its antioxidant and antibacterial properties. Keeping several plants in your space is a great way to establish a positive flow of energy and can absorb, block, and clear any unwanted energies.

SYMBOLS

Symbols are frequently used in amulets and talismans for protective purposes. Many of the symbols we see originate from ancient cultures and traditions. They also stand at the core of our beliefs. Some of these include rosaries, which are a Catholic symbol of protection, and the Helm of Awe, which is a Viking symbol of protection. In many civilizations, attempts to ward off the curse of the evil eye have resulted in a variety of talismans. The nazar is an amulet in the shape of an eye that is said to protect against the evil eye. The hamsa is a hand-shaped charm that Middle Easterners believe will protect them from the evil eye. The evil eye is a curse that is thought to be inflicted by a spiteful gaze that is said to bring bad luck to the person who receives it out of envy or malice.

CHARM BAGS AND WITCH BOTTLES

If you prefer witchcraft, charm bags and witch bottles serve as a craftier version of protection. Although their ingredients vary, to create a charm bag use a cotton cloth and add a small amount of obsidian, dried rosemary, thistle, and black peppercorns.[14]

To make a witch bottle, you will need to fill a glass jar with salt, pins or nails, and vinegar. There are many variations of the witch bottle, like using your own urine instead of vinegar, banishing herbs, other sharp objects, or something from your body such as fingernails and hair, so try what you prefer and find more effective. Hold it in your hands and breathe into it,

---

14. Kelden, *The Crooked Path: An Introduction to Traditional Witchcraft*, (Woodbury, MN: Llewellyn Worldwide Ltd., 2020), 75-79.

once all of the components have been added, experiencing the intrinsic virtues of the materials merging with your own spiritual power to protect you. Place the bottle on your premises and bury it. If burying them in the earth isn't a possibility, they're sometimes concealed in walls or other undisturbed areas of the house. Entities are attracted to them, and they serve as a powerful decoy. The witch bottle is also said to behave like an enemy's bladder producing excruciating pain from the pins, causing the person to stop their ill-wishes.

CRYSTALS

Some examples of protective crystals include black tourmaline, obsidian, and hematite. Charge them by placing them in sunlight for a couple hours and program them by holding them in your dominant hand while setting an intention for protection. Carrying these stones with you can help to protect against negative energy by creating a protective shield. They can also absorb negative energy like a sponge. You may take them anywhere, or place them where you want. Place a programmed crystal in your glove compartment, for example, if you want to be protected while driving. They may also be used to protect yourself from negative ideas. It can assist you in avoiding negative routines and thinking. If you utilize crystals, be sure to cleanse and recharge them on a regular basis. This will aid in the restoration of their normal condition as well as the cleansing of the energy they've absorbed.

BANISHING

Banishing is used for multiple reasons. A banishing is a means of preparing and clearing your environment to let in the energy you desire, as well as providing a protective barrier and removing unwanted energy. Banishing rituals also make you more visible on the spiritual plane so that you can more easily connect with entities and energies. Be mindful that shining brightly on the astral plane also makes you desirable by unwanted energies. This is why performing a banishing before and after spirit work is important. Ending your session with a banishment may also tell spirits firmly and forcefully to leave. Methods and versions vary. They can be performed easily and entirely in the mind, or performed physically in a sacred space, be very elaborate or simple, and require specific tools or nothing but yourself.

The most widely known banishing in the magical community is the LBRP, which stands for Lesser Banishing Ritual of the Pentagram. There are countless resources and even easy-to-follow online tutorials to try if you prefer a visual guide. The LBRP is a ritual that also aims to clear negative energies in your body and sacred space. It can be performed by practitioners with varying levels of experience and expertise. The more I researched, learned, and developed my practice, the more I understood that the LBRP and ritual banishings are less about defense and more about creating a better environment, both internally and energetically, for magic.

First, it's important to note that the LBRP does not offer any worldly rewards and is not considered to be a part of low magic. Happiness, satisfaction, and calm focus, or even purpose in life can absolutely be effects of ceremonial and high magic. However, performing ceremonial magic may include losing a lot of what you may consider important.

A ceremonial magician does not learn the LBRP first in order to be able to quickly banish a demon. If you want more defensive techniques and magic, Damon Brand's *Magical Protection* is an excellent resource. The LBRP is primarily concerned with what you may consider personal demons. It's a purifying process for the practitioner. The LBRP is a temporary rejection of the physical realm in order to give the spiritual realm an opportunity to shine. When working with the LBRP, several practitioners report significant disruptions. Outcomes are always for the practitioner's benefit; however, the process to get there is not always favorable. Such things like the loss of a job or relationship can occur; however, it is to make room for something better. The process isn't always the nicest, and this is why ceremonial magic takes courage and willingness to take a leap of faith.

The LBRP is also an affirmation of a practitioner's place in the universe, and the place of the universe around and within the practitioner. By naming the elements and calling the angels, you send a powerful message to your own subconscious that you are at the center of it all and have agency over it all.

Everything in the universe is an organization of energy, and sometimes we accumulate those energies. Those energies can become stagnant or even malignant. The LBRP allows you to release those energies and make room to introduce new, fresh energy.

The only tools you need for this banishing ritual is yourself, although you may use a dagger or athame instead of pointing with your finger. It can be performed kneeling or standing. Once memorized, this banishing takes four to ten minutes to perform.

Also, for the ritual, you'll need to "vibrate" certain divine names. Vibrating is a method of saying a divine being's name like ingredients of a magical recipe so that it is drawn-out and with a deep, full breath that utilizes the nasal sections to such an extent that the sound feels and sounds "vibrated." Imagine that your voice is being heard at the ends of the universe. This should create a similar sensation as if you were to make a humming sound.

LESSER BANISHING RITUAL OF THE PENTAGRAM

This ritual is best practiced daily. It is used as a barrier that will not only make you more visible on the astral so you can make for a clear connection with the spirits that you wish to, but it will also help prevent unwanted entities from entering your space. This barrier of energy can be as big or small as you intend. It can envelop just you, your entire room, or a house. Perform this banishing before and after any spirit work.

There are different versions of the LBRP in Thelema and Wicca. I will be referring to the Golden Dawn version. The LBRP includes four parts: the Qabalistic Cross, the Pentagrams, Calling the Archangels, and a repeat of the Qabalistic Cross again.

The Qabalistic Cross

The Qabalistic Cross is an invocation of the highest form of divinity. To perform the first part of the ritual, you will need to visualize yourself as the center of the universe with divine light coming through you.

With your eyes closed, visualize a sphere of brilliant white light appearing from above your head. Reach up with your right hand and pull the white light down through your forehead. Say and vibrate the word *AT-AH*. It means "thine is" or "yours is."

Move your finger/wand/athame down to the solar plexus, and as you do this, pay attention to your feet. Imagine a sphere of bright light appearing just between your feet on the ground. Vibrate *MALKUTH* (mahl-koot). It means "the kingdom," and is the lowest sphere on the tree of life. It is the sphere of physical manifestation.

Next, imagine a line of white light running down your body's center, from divinity down to Earth, and touch your right shoulder. Then imagine a shard of white light emanating from your right shoulder. Visualize this beam of light extending to the far reaches of the universe. Vibrate *VE-GEBURAH* (v'ge-boo-rah). It means "and the power." Imagine a similar light as you touch your left shoulder and vibrate *VE-GEDULAH* (v'ge-doo-lah). It means "and the glory." As you touch your left shoulder, visualize a connecting line of white light from your right shoulder to your left that extends out of your body to the outer reaches of the universe. You now have a cross of white light running through you and extending out of each side of you.

Clasp your hands together, as in prayer, in front of your solar plexus and vibrate *LE-OLAHM* (lay-oh-lahm), which means "forever." While saying this, focus on the cross of white light running through you and vibrate *AMEN* (ah-men).

The Pentagrams

Begin by facing east or in the most eastern location of your temple, sacred space, or area. Trace with your finger/wand/athame a large banishing pentagram in the air before you. As you trace each line, visualize the pentagram appearing as intense blue flames.

With your right hand, point to the bottom left direction at hip height, which is the element earth. Trace a line from Earth to above your head, which is spirit. As you point above your head, representing spirit, trace a line of blue flames down, ending to the right at hip height, which represents fire. Trace your finger to your left at about shoulder height to the element air. Trace the pentagram across your body at shoulder height to the right for the element water. Return your finger to the bottom left at hip height to complete the flaming blue pentagram at the element earth.

You are now standing in front of a flaming, bright blue pentagram. As you stand in the east, pierce the center of the pentagram, and as you pierce the pentagram, vibrate *YOD HEH VAV HEH* (yode-heh-vahv-heh).

Keeping your finger or tip of the dagger in the center of your pentagram, turn in a quarter circle to the south and trace a bright white line to the center of the south of your circle. These lines connect your pentagrams.

Trace another pentagram the same way, starting at the bottom left direction at hip height for earth, and once completed, pierce the pentagram's center point and vibrate *ADONAI* (ah-doe-nye).

Keep your right arm out in front of you. Carry the white line of light to the west, repeat the steps of tracing and charging your pentagram, but this time vibrate *EHEIEH* (eh-hey-yay).

Carry the light to the north, trace another pentagram, starting at the bottom left direction at hip height, and once completed, pierce the pentagram's center point and vibrate *AGLA* (ah-gah-la).

Carry the white line of light back to the east, and connect all your pentagrams together. You should now be surrounded by four blue flaming pentagrams in the four equal corners of the circle you've just made. Walk back to the center of your circle and turn to face east.

Calling the Archangels

Extend your arms out and raise your hands on each side of you with palms facing upward. Visualize the Qabalistic Cross you made earlier.

Imagine the four archangels surrounding you. As you face east, look before you and visualize Archangel Raphael, associated with the element air. He appears in yellow robes with purple reflections. Try to feel his presence as though wind is hitting your skin and face and say, "Before me,

RAPHAEL (rah-fay-el)."

Behind you stands Gabriel, associated with the element water, dressed in blue robes with orange reflections. Say, "Behind me, *GABRIEL* (gah-bree-el)," and imagine feeling cool drops of water on your back.

Red represents the element of fire, so imagine Michael dressed in flowing red robes with a flaming sword. Try to feel as though there is heat coming from the sword. Look to your right and say, "On my right, *MICHAEL* (mi-kai-el)."

On your left stands Archangel Uriel. Imagine him holding a pentacle or wheat and dressed in the color of Malkuth from the tree of life, which is olive green, black, ocher, and dark lemon. Look to the left and say, "On my left, *URIEL* (or-ee-el)."

Imagine all four archangels standing outside the circle of flaming blue pentagrams that surround you and say, "For around me flame the pentagrams." Now visualize a column of brilliant bright light shooting up to infinity, through your body, and infinitely downward as a beam of light. If you were to look at the cross section of this light, it would appear as a hexagram. As you imagine this brilliant star column passing through you, say, "And in the column shines the six-ray star."

To finish, simply repeat the steps of the Qabalistic Cross one more time.[15]

Summary

Although psychic protection may not make you entirely impenetrable, remember that it's the people who inadvertently open themselves to harmful energy that are vulnerable, often out of sheer ignorance. It's important to be mindful of your interaction with the spiritual realm and make sure that you are not provoking spirits or making crossed conditions for yourself. The term *crossed* refers to the spiritual condition where an individual is in a continually blocked or hexed state. Crossing can happen when you constantly speak negatively about yourself. It can also occur if you pass

---

15. Kraig, Donald M, "Lesser Banishing Ritual of the Pentagram," Llewellyn Worldwide, Accessed July 21, 2020, https://www.llewellyn.com/encyclopedia/article/5139.

through sacred places where you're unwelcome, or through locations that have been imprinted with particularly nasty energies. Crossing can also happen if you are on the receiving end of intense hatred and rage either from a person or a spirit.

A protective measure that is so often overlooked and underutilized is setting boundaries. There are many reasons why someone might not want to work with a spirit or not want the energy in their space. So it's important to vocally and clearly explain why an entity is not welcome or why you are creating certain boundaries. Be respectful and remain calm, but be firm and confident in your conviction. It is your space and your life, and you have the right to claim it.

Some entities may require a peace offering. If you feel they may be offended, you can leave them a token of gratitude for leaving your space and respecting your boundaries. Do not invite them into your home by placing the offering inside your space. Instead, leave the offering outside, or, if you can, at a place away from your property. State who it's for and why you are leaving it. Follow up with a cleansing and banishing ritual.

For whatever reason, if you want to get rid of spirits, rest assured that you are more than capable. There is no reason for you to be afraid of spirits. Be confident in knowing that you have all the power and aptitude that you need.

Chapter 8

CENTERING, SHIELDING, AND GROUNDING

I briefly touched on centering and its importance to connect with the spirit realm, but the root of it is to provide a foundation in order to access the mental state to tap into energy. Centering and meditation share many similarities, especially in their methodology, so if you know how to center, it can help immensely with getting into a meditative state. Depending on your traditions or your magical practice, centering may be referred to by another name and definition—feel free to explore and try some different centering techniques. If you feel compelled, try different ones to find what is aligned with your practice.

CENTERING

Centering doesn't need to be difficult or overly complicated. The secret to receptivity for spiritual communication is presence achieved through centering. We can center ourselves by focusing on our breath to relax and create a space or a presence for energy reception or to hear energetic messages.

The goal here is to achieve a state where you feel relaxed and calm. Find a space that is comfortable and free from any distractions. Once you are in a comfortable seated position, close your eyes and focus on your breathing. Begin by taking a deep breath and feel where the breath expands in your body. As you breathe in, count it as one and inhale. Hold it for a few seconds and count it as one and exhale. Continue breathing in and out holding for a couple seconds and continue this pattern of counting. Count two and inhale, count two and exhale. Now, count to three as you continue to inhale and exhale to regulate your breathing. Bring your attention and focus to your counting and feeling where in your body the breath expands so you may clear your mind of any intruding or distracting thoughts. As you reach the count of five, you should be breathing evenly. Notice if there is a stillness and void in your mind. If you get to five and still receive distracting thoughts or have an overactive mind, begin again counting your breath at one. The more often you practice this, the easier it becomes.

Once you can feel the sensation of being present and a clear, empty space in front of you, visualize energy in your heart space growing and swirling like a brilliant glowing ball of light. Practice seeing the energy in your mind, growing and expanding to encompass and envelop your entire body. Allow this energy to rest within your core, send it up, and send it out. Visualize feeling and seeing that you are shooting this energy out to the farthest reaches of the cosmos. You are now ready to set intentions and ask your spirit guides to come close. The process of sending this energy out makes you visible on the spiritual plane so that your intentions may be heard and so you can receive clearly from your guides.

Every time you center, you'll begin by repeating this process, first by focusing on your breath and visualizing energy in your heart. Centering becomes stronger and easier the more you practice it. Eventually, you'll be able to center anywhere at any time.

SHIELDING

Shielding is a technique of energy work where you envelop yourself, a space, or an object in protective energy. A shield is created by a combination of setting your intention of blocking any unwanted energies and visualizing the energy expanding from you to work in your favor. First, you'll need to center. Just focus on your inner energy either from your heart or solar plexus like you did in the centering exercise. Think about or say out loud who or what you want to shield. Now visualize and try feeling as though your energy core is expanding outward, surrounding you and hardening to form a shell. This shell of energy forms a hard and reflective surface, impenetrable and repelling anything negative back to where it came from. The same process can be practiced for objects and spaces. Some people visualize their shield as a protective bubble; others see it as a hardened shell or as a second layer of impenetrable, diamond-like skin. However you visualize your energetic shield, knowing and believing that it is effective will make it so.

When the time comes that a psychic shield is no longer needed, you may want to lower or remove it. This is a simple process as well and requires only your thoughts and intention to manipulate the energy. To lower a shield, all you need to do is think about the shield disappearing and then try to feel or visualize it lowering and disintegrating.

GROUNDING

Grounding is a technique that should be performed after working with any energy or spirit work. It's a method of regulating yourself back to a state of normalcy. When we work with spirits and invisible energy, we often tap into their power and can unintentionally absorb energy, thoughts, and emotions that aren't our own. Grounding helps alleviate the effects of energy work so your energy is your own. Grounding is simple enough. When we center and shield, we draw and expand energy; when we ground, we release any excess energy. Grounding activities vary, but no matter how mundane they seem, it's a practice that should never be overlooked or disregarded. Methods of grounding are your choice. They can be anything from having a snack to listening to music. Grounding should be a task that brings your consciousness back to the present state and pushes excess energy into something else.[16]

Earthing is one of the most popular methods to ground yourself. Earthing is simple and enjoyable. Remove your shoes and walk outside so

16. Wigington, Patti, "Magical Grounding, Centering, and Shielding Techniques," Learn Religions, accessed Mar 30, 2021, https://www.learnreligions.com/grounding-centering-and-shielding-4122187.

that your feet make direct contact with the earth. Some claim that earthing is less effective if they stand on cement or substances that prevent direct contact with their feet and the earth. Do what feels right to you; allow for the energy to flow out of you. As you focus on the energy, gain control of it and visualize expelling it from you. Visualize it like water made of light, pouring out of you and draining away. You can also try picturing as though roots are growing down through your legs and anchoring into the earth. Visualize the flow of energy from the earth circulating, healing, and clearing away any excess.

If you can't walk outside for whatever reason and would prefer to push out any excess energy into something else, close your eyes and picture having control over it. Visualize the energy coming out of your hands and let the earth or an object absorb it. You can also ground with crystals and stones and let them absorb energy you no longer need. Trees and plants also work very well to absorb and transmit energy.

You have to remember that for the majority of practitioners, grounding is actually second nature, and we, more often than not, do things already that keep us grounded without even realizing it. Bathing, eating a snack, drinking water, or going outside and connecting with nature are all methods most of us do frequently, if not daily. In some instances, protective measures such as spiritual grounding are often overemphasized, when, in fact, you are already protected and generally already follow your own version of these techniques as a part of your routine or habits. Grounding should be a reminder that when we do not feel like ourselves, when our energy is drained or needs to be reclaimed and, essentially, we need to connect back to this plane of reality.

The point being, do not allow yourself to fall into listening to naysayers who tell you to make sure you are protecting yourself. This may cause adverse effects, or the opposite of what you are trying to achieve, like apprehension or fear, when you already are protected. Protective practices are safeguards, and it's important to make a habit of them if you are constantly using spiritual techniques that take your consciousness out of your physical body. Simply put, protective measures like grounding are for reconnecting us to the mundane.

In addition, everyone has spirit guides, and most of us who aren't actively seeking to work in their opposition will remain under their protection. Our spiritual teams are working to protect us from any actual spiritual harm, like gatekeepers who allow contact with only benevolent forces, unless you consciously or subconsciously negate their protection. Although it is important to seize control over your will and your mind so you don't accidentally cause negativity to come into your life. The majority of us are, in fact, protected without being fully aware of it.

Chapter 9

ACCESSING THE SPIRIT REALMS

If you share an interest in the occult or supernatural, chances are you've seen or heard about the pineal gland. Throughout its documentation, the pineal gland is also referred to as the witch's eye, third eye, or mind's eye. It's a small pea-shaped gland in the brain, and its spiritual function can be relative to accessing unseen energy. By scientific standards, the pineal gland is responsible for producing and regulating hormones based on the information received from the light-dark cycle—the periodic pattern of light (artificial or natural) alternating with darkness—of a person's environment.

From metaphysics, the pineal gland has strong associations with the sixth chakra. In the seventeenth century, René Descartes described and regarded it as the seat of the soul and where thoughts are formed. It's believed to be responsible for the development of intuition, decisiveness, personal evolution, and helps balance our energy on the physical and spiritual planes.

As you begin to attune to the invisible energies around you, you may begin to start noticing things that you aren't sure actually exist, or wonder if your mind is playing tricks on you. Don't worry, this is perfectly normal; you are noticing things that were there all along but were unable to access them. As the third eye opens or activates, you may also experience increased pressure around your head or between your eyebrows. Some people may begin experiencing seeing energies on the physical plane with their eyes, often as orbs of light, and others may see them in their mind, commonly referred to as "inner sight." Some people recognize a faint high-pitched ringing in their ears as they begin to attune to invisible energies. Whether you experience energy physically or intuitively, both experiences are just as real.

People are drawn to spirit work for all types of reasons. They may seek out spirits for assistance to heal themselves or to provide answers to life's mysteries. Regardless of your reasons, beliefs, and practices, spirit work can benefit everyone, but only if you are open to it. Fears and doubts will create a veil that will prevent the clarity of possibilities. First, you must trust that you are learning this sacred art for a reason.

As you begin to develop your intuition, activate your third eye, and attune to the invisible energies and entities, you will be connected to it for life. Practitioners who put in the prework and foundation of attuning to these energies with intuitive development is what ultimately makes them capable of maintaining relationships with spirits. Creating this foundation establishes an appropriate channel for the flow of energy and energetic messages. Try meditating each day for a week as you practice your development and attuning. Meditating each day during the process allows for a clearer focus on your thoughts and expectations on becoming a channel for energy. Essentially, you're turning yourself into a wireless receiver capable of tuning into universal energies that constantly surround us.

THIRD EYE ACTIVATION EXERCISE

Although there are various strategies for activating and further opening or decalcifying the third eye, I've found that using crystals is one of the most successful. The vibration of a crystal tends to amplify a person's energetic vibrational frequency, which can speed up or accelerate the effects of intention and visualization.

For this technique, you will need two amethyst or lapis lazuli crystals. It's important to work with crystals that match your vibration and intention. These crystals are common examples used in the healing and mystical arts for boosting psychic energy. However, if you feel more inclined to work with another, please do so.

Cleanse your crystals before you begin. Cleansing can be done by placing them in saltwater, with smoke, sound, or if the crystals are buried in the ground for a few hours. Although I've never had any issues with cleansing these crystals with water, some people warn against lapis' prolonged contact with water because it may dissolve and damage the calcite content, which is true for a lot of crystals ending with "ite." After cleansing, place a crystal in each hand. If your crystal has a point, be sure to create a circuit. Simply disregard this step if your crystals are not pointed. To create a circuit, place one crystal in your left hand with the point facing toward you and one in the right hand with the point facing away from you.

Close your eyes and focus on your breath. With each breath in, visualize and intend a positive bright light and energy coming in through the crystals. Allow it to penetrate your body, move through your arm to your heart and up to your third eye (between your eyebrows), healing and purifying it. Now visualize it clearing away and removing any toxicity or blocks as an energy leaving your body from your third eye and exiting out of your right hand through the crystal. As the energy exits and hits the crystal, the energy is cleansed and transformed back to pure light as it's released. With each breath in, continue to visualize a beautiful white light of energy entering through your left-hand crystal and up through your heart to your third eye. This energy removes blockages and buildup, cleansing and clearing them out of you as it moves down through your right-hand side and out of your body through the crystal. Continue visualizing this energy flow for three to five minutes. You may play 963 Hz sounds or music to help you into a meditative state. This exercise can be repeated as many times as you feel necessary, but remember to cleanse your crystals after each session.

Affirm the following during this process:

"I am open to the flow of pure spiritual energy to cleanse my third eye."
"As the pure and radiant energy passes through my body, all blockages are removed."
"My third eye is cleansed, healed, and activated."

Alternatively, if you don't have any crystals, begin by playing 963 Hz sounds or music to help you into a meditative state. Once you are relaxed and can clearly visualize a bright spiritual light radiating above you, allow it to flow down into you through your crown chakra, through the top of your head. Feel the love and gratitude toward this beautiful spiritual energy. As it flows through the top of your head, it moves into your third eye, purifying and healing it. Continue this exercise for eleven minutes. The number one is associated with beginnings and new energy. The number eleven is a master number, commanding extra power in the universe due to the pairing of the same number. It is a sign of both incredible mental and physical power, including heightened intuition, increased psychic abilities, and sensitivity.

As you strengthen your bonds and your skills with the other side, you may experience sounds or images that aren't coming from the physical world. By opening or closing the floodgates, you control how much information flows in. If you wish for more information, visualize large heavy doors made of a brilliant and almost blinding light that block the entrance and a massive lake that is sparkling with radiant beautiful energy. These doors are controlled by a lever you hold on to. As you push the lever forward, the doors swing open more and the light energy flows like water through the top of your head and connects with your heart and inner current. If you pull the lever back, the immense and heavy doors close, severing the flow of this water like glowing energy.

Most people will be adept at developing at least one of the clair (clear) psychic senses, and some people can master several, but most often people don't know which one because psychic senses generally tend to be dormant. It's like never having used a specific part of your body; it would become atrophied. To develop your psychic sense, it's a matter of becoming aware of which sense you have a talent for and learning how to discern that energetic information. It all begins with reading and researching about the clair senses and determining what fits and is aligned with you through discernment, intuition, and process of elimination, and then practicing to develop it.

You won't do any harm if you practice being clairaudient if you actually have a stronger clairsentient ability. Clairsentience is a term for when people gain intuitive knowledge in the form of feelings and emotions. They may be able to hear messages and communications in other instances, which is known as clairaudience. You're going to strengthen psychic senses through practicing, so if you don't know which sense you are more capable of, try practicing them all. Its effectiveness and your progress of development begin with believing and shutting out any doubts or fears. In chapter fourteen I'll discuss the psychic senses more in-depth.

Chapter 10

SPIRITUAL RELATIONSHIPS

By now you're familiar with how to protect yourself against negative energies and entities, how spirits communicate with us, and how to adhere to proper guidelines of practice to remain in their good graces. You may be wondering why you'd want a relationship with a spirit at all, or if having a team of spirit allies is worth all the time and effort. Spirits are powerful; some are capable of pretty much anything and can fulfill any desire or wish. Experienced practitioners don't just randomly pick an entity to work with to fulfill a task—that's because most spirits have a specialty that grants them specific abilities. Just like how certain professions specialize in an area of expertise, such as a psychologist or a financial advisor, some spirits are excellent at coaching you to achieve your full potential, and others are more adept at helping you to manifest wealth. If you are going to form relationships with spirits and ask for their help, don't pick just any spirit. Research to find out what they specialize in and if they show traits or a demeanor you would prefer to connect with. If you don't want to work with a spirit that shows characteristics of being short-tempered and spiteful, be mindful not to invoke it.

⚹ It is your choice which spirits you want to work with, although spirits often pick us too. When a spirit wants to initiate a connection with you, it is often referred to as "a calling." There are many reasons why a spirit may want to connect with you—they might just like you or believe that you could benefit from its help. Other reasons for a spirit's motivation to seek a connection with you could be love; it may be an ancestor or guardian. They could just be a very generous spirit, or they recognize a need they can fulfill in exchange for veneration and gifts. Sometimes it's their duty and responsibility to help people. But in order for a spirit to provide their assistance, they must be aware of your need, and upon delivery or fulfillment, they require some sort of credit in return. Failure to hold up your end of the bargain will often result in a spirit's admonishment, withdrawal, or departure. To put it another way, nothing comes for free.

IDENTIFYING SPIRITS

Some good indicators that a spirit is close by is when you constantly hear their name, can't stop thinking about them, and have impeding thoughts or images linking to them. Whatever it may be, the energy that is near you will often cause you to feel drawn to wanting to discover more. Stronger relationships with spirits can be formed in similar ways to how we develop our human friendships. When you establish common ground and similar interests, or share mutual admiration and traits, there's usually a natural inclination to connect with them and vice versa.[17]

Some spirits are not always met in the comfort of your sacred space, and if you seek to connect with a particular archetype, you may be required to visit them in a neutral setting where they like to gather. If you're seeking an engagement with spirits and are not ready to invite them into your space, then perhaps begin by visiting them at crossroads and thresholds. These natural intersections and convergences of energy are active places for meeting spirits.

Spirits can gather in physical or spiritual instances of meeting grounds. The reason why these places are so active with spirits is because they emit intense and powerful energies that spirits crave. Their presence in these places also contributes to the magnitude of energy. Spirits are highly active at thresholds and crossroads. Unlike crossroads, which maintain a point of

---

17. Illes, Judika, *Encyclopedia Of Spirits*, (New York, NY: HarperCollins Publishers, 2009), 21-23.

intersection, thresholds contain the space of bordering elements or ener-gies. For instance, a shoreline where land meets sea would be considered a threshold. A spiritual example of thresholds are cemeteries and delivery rooms—considered thresholds of life and death.

Other examples of where we can connect with spirits include their shrines and temples. Shrines and temples can be man-made or natural. Natural shrines may develop in something like a spring or tree, and the portals are often opened because of intense concentration and continued patronage. Energy follows thoughts. Spirits are often contacted to come forward by giving them attention and intense focus. Acts of reverence often generate spirit interactions. You may please a spirit by providing a home for them such as planting them a tree or constructing an altar.

Spirits may appear in many forms. I had a profound experience meet-ing my spirit guide for the first time on the astral plane. Upon setting the intention of meeting my spirit guide and following a guided medita-tion, she appeared as a tall and blue-skinned alien. She was bald except for a tiara-like band across her forehead. Although human-like, she was very slender and her extremities seemed stretched. I don't remember her speaking, but there was a clear feeling. All I could feel was immense love emanating from her. Her energy was maternal and compassionate. There was a clear feminine energy that I felt coming from her. At the time, I had very little information about alien spirits which I refer to as star or cosmic beings. One day I was scrolling online, and came across a picture of a blue skinned bald alien with pointy ears that stopped me in my tracks. It was the closest artistic depiction of the spirit guide that I met and confirmed my belief in our capability to have a spiritual connection with beings who are not human.

Although my experience with my guide was very positive, there is a reason why one does not rush into working with more powerful entities such as deities until we understand how spirits appear and how they com-municate. Visions, messages, and communication with spirits and dei-ties are most commonly experienced on the astral and in deep meditative states. Only after you are familiar with working and channeling human energies or spirit guides should you attempt to reach deities. The reason for this is that, like angels and demons, deities are incredibly powerful energies, devoid of human traits and emotions. They do not think like us, nor act like us, and certainly do not look like us. Spirit guides and ancestors are much more forgiving because they generally care about us and communicate in ways that are more familiar.

Personified traits were given to deities by humans, but they are far from human. In order to help people connect with and establish a more rational relationship, we put a face to the energy so people may fear them less and simplify devotional acts like paying tribute.

I have a cautionary tale about working with deities. When I wasn't entirely prepared, meeting a deity was a frightening event, at least in my situation. After I had spent some time working with and venerating my matron deity, she appeared to me on the astral in a deep meditation. Visiting the astral realm is like a lucid dream for me. I was conscious of my surroundings and in command of my actions. However, there were no surroundings in this case, only a dark abyss. A massive green snake emerged out of the void, not slithering on the ground but standing upright and towering above me. If you like snakes, this experience could have been a little less frightening for you; however, I was frozen in fear.

When the snake leaned forward toward me, I decided to take this as a chance to demonstrate my bravery and thought that I should not be terrified of its appearance, so I extended my hand in an attempt to pat the snake. This was a tremendous error that I discovered later.

Assume you're traveling to a distant nation where you don't speak the language. What methods do you use to communicate with the locals? You probably utilize gestures and point to symbols, signs, and other items, as well as use motions and body language. The same is true if a spirit appears to you and speaks to you in a language other than your first language or native speech. Pay attention to their body language and any other means of communication they use. Deities frequently appear in the shape of creatures with whom they are linked, and they rarely talk when in this form.

My matron diety bowed forward as a greeting, and as a misunderstanding, I impolitely and ignorantly tried to pat her head. In this case, a courteous bow would be the appropriate response as a sign of respect and greeting. Up until then, I was granted any desire I petitioned her for in exchange for my devotion. For example, I once petitioned her for help to increase the number of my supporters, admirers and patrons. Shortly after that number grew exponentially. After our interaction on the astral plane, she did not fulfill my petitions. No matter what I asked my matron deity for and no matter how great the offering, it did not come to fruition. All I could do was humbly gesture and ask for forgiveness in order to reclaim her grace and love. Apologizing and asking for forgiveness usually includes some form of an offering. Sometimes a spirit may forgive a devotee and reconnect with them, and sometimes the damage has already been done, so it will not.

How did I know it was my matron deity when she appeared as a snake and didn't speak? Apart from my claircognizant ability and trusting my inner knowledge, I discovered that snakes are sacred to her. Conducting considerable study before forming a connection with her was integral. My intuition informed me she wasn't an animal spirit because of her massive size and demeanor, as well as the fact that I hadn't established the intention or called on any animal spirits beforehand. Everything pointed to my matron, from the signs and timing to the work and intentions I had established.

To help you identify a spirit, pay attention to what you are doing, what your intentions are beforehand, who you are consciously or purposefully asking to connect with, and what you have asked the universe for at the time you meet a spirit. Accurately identifying spirits is a combination of using common sense, critical thinking, research, listening to your intuition, and the process of elimination. You may not be met on the astral plane by spirits, but they may visit us in different ways, such as in dreams or providing synchronicities. If you need to identify a spirit, begin by considering all the spirits it could be and eliminate who it isn't by determining what characteristics are unlike them.

When in doubt, you can use divination, or ask for signs of confirmation for validation. Lean into the feeling of knowing by trusting your instincts. Spirits often send us signs or symbols to confirm their identity.

BUILDING A RELATIONSHIP WITH A SPIRIT

To build a relationship with a spirit, begin by identifying who is close by or who you wish to connect with. The only certain way to determine who they are is by researching and cross-checking, and then tuning in to your intuition to see if that spirit resonates with you.

Whether you choose to reach out to a deity or ancestor spirit, researching them to understand more about their personality and their preferences for interaction, including proper etiquette and communication methods, will help you maintain and strengthen your bond. That's to say good manners and respect go a long way in building a relationship.

The next step is to perform a cleansing and dedicate an area you wish to connect to and communicate with them. This will help to clear the energy and manifest a portal for spirit interaction. Your sacred space can be as plain as setting out a single candle or decorating it with imagery and items that help to connect you to them. Focus and concentrate on the spirit and envision how they make you feel. For example, if you want them to help you with your communication skills so you can get a promotion, try feeling the gratitude and appreciation toward the spirit as if you've already received the promotion. The spirit may help you in other ways like providing opportunities when you least expect them, or aligning you with a career that is more suited to your best interest and higher soul's purpose. In exchange, you'll need to tend to your relationship and feed them or give them credit for their assistance.

In order to feed a spirit in exchange for their service, you can provide offerings. Since spirits do not have a physical body, they cannot consume or use physical things the way we do. In this case, when you present a physical offering to a spirit you must carry over its energetic vibration to the spirit realm by visualizing it there. Offerings are not always physical. They can be devotional acts of kindness, or messages and provisions carrying energetic vibrations to provide a spirit with love, devotion, and gratitude. Regard offerings as an act of love and respect.

Malefic entities crave energy, often from fear, but benevolent ones seek an exchange of positive energy. Love is one of the most powerful and protective ingredients in connecting with a spirit. Whether you choose to connect to an ancestor or deity, be mindful of the type of offering you are making. They should be made as a gesture of respect and honor. Ancestors may prefer things that they once enjoyed in their human life, while deities respond well to known associations based on their folklore and mythology. If you choose to work with Athena, for instance, she responds well to creative projects or the fruits of your labor because she is a goddess of crafts. Research will help you indicate which offerings are more suitable and preferred by the spirit you wish to connect with. Although you may not find exact or specified examples, use your discernment and intuition. In most cases, as long as you provide offerings with an air of reverence, they tend to be regarded and accepted. When in doubt, clean water is a fairly universal example.

Upon initial contact with a spirit, it's important that they know who you are and what your intentions are. The polite and respectful thing to do would be to introduce yourself, let them know who you wish to connect with and why. This is also good practice for protection and allows for only spirits that have your best interest at heart to manifest. When setting an intention of connecting to spirits, make sure you are removed from any anxiety, anger, or negative feelings to be sure to connect with love and keep away any negative energies and entities. Give the spirit time to manifest. Listen to see if you receive feelings of their presence, receive imagery, or hear messages. Sometimes a spirit's answer and presence may come later, at a time when they can be perceived more clearly.

Total relaxation often provides the necessary state to be receptive to energetic messages and allow us to open to the flow of energy. If you do not hear a response or receive confirmation immediately, do not be discouraged. It doesn't mean your efforts are unanswered. They simply might need time to coordinate appropriate communication. A spirit guide will often communicate to you in the format you resonate with, and their messages may come now or much later. This can be in many kinds of formats, imagery, sounds, signs, or synchronicities to which you recognize. The environmental conditions need to be right to allow for clarity, otherwise communication may be muddled and misunderstood.

After you've introduced yourself, established a connection, and paid your respects, then it's time to end the ritual and say goodbye. To politely bid them farewell, express your appreciation and gratitude for them. You may ask them to leave or invite them to stay; however, be absolutely sure you know who the spirit is and clarify their intentions.

When you work with spirits, it's important to maintain appropriate boundaries. Ensure that you are clear what you seek and what they require in exchange. Some spirits will be willing to negotiate, others will not. If at any time you are uncomfortable with the conditions of your partnership, it is your choice to either continue with them or take a step back. Setting boundaries may include things like establishing a specific length of time you wish to work with them. For instance, you may choose to work with a spirit during a holiday that is evocative for a stronger connection. It may include petitioning them for a certain task, like protection as you travel abroad. Upon your return you can either choose to continue the relationship or withdraw.

Remember, committing to a relationship with spirits is a serious and long-term endeavor. Make sure you know who it is you're connecting with by proper identification through research. Clearly establish appropriate intentions in regard to the type, traits, or characteristics of the spirit you want to work with. Spirits are often specialists, so be selective and discerning when working with them. Establishing a healthy and respectful partnership with a spirit can share similar qualities to that of a human relationship.

Communicating boundaries, reciprocating generosity, love, and kindness, and maintaining mutual respect will strengthen and form long-lasting spirit allies. Consider carefully before proceeding with any rituals to connect with spirits or before choosing to invite them into your life. Be conscious of and cautious of the severity of encouraging spirits to become a part of your life. The benefits can be plenty but are not to be taken lightly. Think long and hard before contacting a spirit and the reasons you have for doing so—disrespect can have severe consequences if you petition spirits in this manner. You may need to reconsider and seek another way of getting what you desire before asking for their assistance.

Chapter 11

METHODS OF COMMUNICATION AND PETITIONING

All over the world, for many millennia, people of different cultures and groups have been petitioning and communicating with spirits. Although details like the type of food offered or the scent of incense might vary, the core methods and formats in which people connect with spirits have remained. The Fox sisters' celebratory status helped launch the spiritual movement in the late nineteenth century. These three women communicated with spirits by asking questions and listening to rapping on the wall for answers. Today, communication from spirits comes to us in many ways, including signs, symbols, and dreams, and often involves some sort of exchange as a token of gratitude and recognition. The fundamentals of independent spirit work are universal; however, individual beliefs, including desires, fears, needs, or level of compulsion and emotions, will affect the result of the transaction.

Before you begin practicing the different methods of communicating, let's revisit some basics. First, cleanse before you begin so you set the intent of connecting with only the energies you want to. A sacred space should always be clean and tidy before inviting new energies in and ensures clearing out any unwanted energy so you don't unintentionally connect to something less desirable. Use smoke, a cleansing wash, or choose your own favorite cleansing method before attempting contact with spirits.

Take precautions against any negative energies and entities. Safeguarding against picking up unwanted entities and energies helps limit the negative influences they can have on our lives. It's always better to be safe than sorry, but there's no need to overdo it. Using your preferred protective methods in the appropriate way and with proper intention will always do the trick.

Be conscious of who you're connecting with. Don't invite conversations with every spirit or entity. Although instances of contact with spirits who cause actual harm are rare, there are those that exist who don't always consider your best interests. The best way to protect yourself from vulnerability is to clearly state who it is you are welcoming to connect with. If you feel uncomfortable or sense negative energy, tell them firmly and politely to leave. Setting boundaries will help provide you with self-preservation and keep any unwanted energies away. It gets much easier recognizing which spirits are loving and altruistic the longer you spend time building your relationships.

Lastly, use your common sense. Don't purposefully put yourself in harm's way. Also, realize that just like humans, spirits who care about us may not always tell us the truth. Sometimes spirits will keep things hidden from us for our own benefit or share incorrect information out of sincerity or concern. Keep using your discernment, critical thinking, and cross-checking skills. Whatever the case is, remember you are an intelligent person capable of recognizing misinformation and red flags. Continue to question things and be diligent about double-checking when you feel it's necessary.

ALTARS

Communication with spirits is unlimited. While some people inherit certain strengths with psychic abilities, others find meditating at a location of centralized energy particularly conducive to aid their communicative efforts. Altars serve many purposes throughout many various practices and traditions. In terms of communicating with spirits, creating an altar establishes a protective space to connect with spirits and exchange energy with them, which aids in building a stronger and long-lasting relationship.

Although altar purposes may vary, like dedicating a space to work with a spirit or for setting specific intentions and performing rituals, their setup and appearance is as vast as the practitioners that work with them. They can be elaborate or simple, but a successful altar comes down to choosing which items you connect with to represent or dedicate to certain energies, intentions, and spirits. The space you build an altar in should feel comfortable and removed from distraction. Altars also serve as a portal for spirits and are a powerful way to build a clear channel of energy. Focusing intensely on the energy you wish to connect with at an altar can have very positive results in manifesting outcomes. Consciously tending to your altar through petitioning spirits in exchange for your devotion encourages success. Furthermore, it can have tremendous benefits, as long as you remember to listen to your instincts and intuition.

SYMBOLS & SYNCHRONICITIES

Signs are just one of the many forms through which spirits try to communicate with us. Physical signs are one of the primary indications that spirits are trying to contact us and send us a message. Signs from spirits can come in many forms, including physical signs, symbols, or synchronicities. They can hold a vast potential of meanings, but signs from spirits hold a significance to the person it's intended for.

You'll recognize signs because of your connection to them. Spirits will more often use items that resonate with you either consciously or subconsciously. Synchronicities are similar in the sense that you'll feel like it's something familiar or receive a déjà vu kind of moment. A synchronicity is an occurrence of events that are random but appear to have relevant or significant meaning.

To receive signs from spirits that you have a connection with, be clear on your request and to whom, as well as what it is you recognize as a sign. You can also tell spirits which items are important to you and ask them to provide a sign for guidance or clarity.

When something resembling a message comes your way, focus on your thoughts and what was happening at the time. The meaning might come to you later, or it might already be embedded into your subconscious to later be accessed. Feel that it is connected with you to provide answers or messages from beyond this plane of existence, without wishing it to be but knowing it is.

If you think you haven't received signs, it may indicate that the meaning may not come to you instantly but later at a time when you need to access its meaning. Be patient—the meaning can come at any time, including minutes or weeks later. Spirits and the universe are constantly sending us signs. If you feel like you received a spiritual sign, but you're not entirely sure what it means, try this affirmation: *"I send gratitude to my guides and the universe for this, and I release needing to know what it means at this time because its meaning will become clear to me when I need it."*

There may be many symbols that become your own. With time, you will learn to recognize when a thing is either a symbol for you or meaningful to someone else's life. Certain things have become the universal symbols of spiritual communication.

- Bells indicate marriage or a celebratory event.
- Candles on a cake often mean a birthday.
- White clouds represent joy, while dark clouds are for loss or hardship.
- A key represents success or achievement.
- Letters are indicative of new messages or announcements.
- Specks of light are often associated with spiritual development.
- A bright light is usually a spirit with a message.
- Cradles signify childbirth.
- Money is reflective of prosperity, abundance, or literal cash flow.
- Rainbows are prosperous and signify joy.
- Roses are for love or friendship.
- Wishbones represent a wish fulfillment.
- Blue or purple commonly refer to spirituality.
- Red is reflective of temper or experiencing passion.
- Yellow is reflective of needing or going through changes.
- Orange represents feelings of joy.

• Pink represents being in love or acquiring good health.

• Green represents wealth or feeling envious.[18]

The meaning always comes clearly if you trust that it will and allow for your path to run its course. Seeing signs in your everyday life that confirm your spiritual experiences can be incredibly powerful.

MEDITATION

Meditation is vital and necessary to access the door to the other side. When it comes to meditation, the first rule of thumb is this: there is no singular or correct way to meditate. The most beneficial environment to establish accurate and strong connections with spirits is a state of relaxation. Relaxation establishes the necessary receptivity to clearly connect with spirits and energies. Meditation methods vary—from using dance, movement, and drumbeats to practicing stillness and breath work. To find out what best puts you in a meditative state, try as many methods as possible to see which format suits you best. The goal with meditation is to create a space in the mind for clarity. Meditation can be the means to bring you answers as well as provide the foundation to meet spirits.

Prior to commencing your meditation, state what your desired outcome is. You can do this as a prayer, or simply by stating, "With this meditation, I seek to… [state your intention]." Then begin your meditation by whichever method you prefer. There is a plethora of guided meditations available online that are great for beginners.

When my overactive mind won't allow me to get into a meditative state, grounding or performing some sort of active movement and exercise helps to expel excess energy before I begin. I've also enjoyed entering meditative states while walking or dancing. There is no limit to the formats of meditation, but you'll want to choose somewhere that is comfortable and free from any distractions. Try things like diffusing lavender essential oil, using calming crystals like lepidolite, lighting candles, or wearing comfortable clothing. The goal here is to quiet the conscious mind of

---

18. Buckland, Raymond, *Buckland's Book of Spirit Communications*, (Woodbury, MN: Llewellyn, 2008), 67-68.

impeding thoughts so that you allow for your answers to come through clearly. This state cannot be achieved through force. Although it's nearly impossible to relinquish and subdue all impeding thoughts, just allow for them to come and pass. The goal here is to work on achieving a state of relaxation—the state right before you enter sleep—and you may do so by any methods that work for you.

If you're having trouble meditating, begin by asking yourself what helps you to get into the state of relaxation? Is it listening to calming sounds and music? Is it counting down from 1,000? Do what works for you. Regular practice will help strengthen your skill and help you better understand the place you are trying to get to in your mind. Don't chase thoughts. When you are completely relaxed, witness them entering your mind and allow them to pass. What images do you see? What do you hear? The messages and answers you seek can enter your mind in various different ways. Simply accept that the answer you are looking for is here, without wishing but knowing it to be.

AUTOMATIC WRITING

Automatic writing is used to produce words without the use of the conscious mind. That is, writing that uses the unconscious energies through a practitioner's or medium's hand and arm to communicate. As you hold the pen or pencil over the paper, your hand will make small movements. These will then cause marks on the paper. At first, these marks are just swirls and lines. Over time, they become more and more consecutive, forming letters and words. One of the advantages of automatic writing is that it is done virtually anywhere. Just sit down and take a sheet of paper with you while you read a book or watch television.

This is a form of spiritual contact where you can connect directly with the spirits and write down messages from them. Often, the writing will appear in the spirit's handwriting style. Automatic writing is one form of spiritual contact that you'll want to focus your mind on something else entirely while performing. This is where your hand will be able to write a message without focusing on what is being written. Some people believe that using your nondominant hand is better for automatic writing.

To channel a message from a spirit, you will need to write a note with a notebook and a pen or pencil, as well as enter a light trance state. Use trance triggers such as incense or shamanic drumming. Protect yourself by creating a space that only one spirit can enter at a time, either by warding or shiedling.

PATHWORKING

Pathworking is a type of meditation that allows you to experience the spirit world psychically while still tied to your physical body. Pathworking is a process where you follow a path that leads to the spirit world and back again to where you came from. The key elements are a clear entrance and an exit point, making it easier for your consciousness to return. A good entry/exit point can be anywhere. You can use a door, a tree, a cave, or a mountaintop. What's most important is that you've got a recognizable and easy-to-find path back. Before you start a journey, make a rough road map. This will help you identify your goal, entry/exit points, and a general idea of where you're going. Pathworking is relatively beginner friendly, and I recommend starting with it before trying astral travel. Even if you are more advanced, pathworking is still a great option because it's often easier to perform than astral travel.

How to journey with pathworking

Before you begin, establish a goal and a rough road map. You can use a candle to purify the room or use a ritual broom to sweep away old energy. Sitting or lying down can help you start meditating. You can also use music or breathing techniques to help you reach a state of deep relaxation. Once you've reached a meditative state, you'll see yourself standing at an entry point into the astral realm.

Return to the entry/exit point once you've completed your journey or your question is answered. This step will help you get back to your physical state. Once you are fully aware and back on the physical plane, remember to use a grounding method. If you choose, record your pathworking experience to reflect on later.

Pathworking Exercise

For this exercise, we'll be working with benevolent spirits and asking your spirit guides to come close and meet you in your sacred space. Once you are comfortable and confident with this ritual, feel free to customize it to your will with guidance from your intuition. Eventually, you may choose another archetype to invite into your ritual. For example, if you wish to call upon an ancestor, you may play their favorite song, or recite lines from their favorite book. The options are endless, just make it personal. Keep in mind, recording this meditation for playback can make following along easier and for a less interrupted experience.

If you choose to provide a physical offering like food or water, place it in its offering dish or on the altar when you begin. If it's an energetic offering, state out loud what it is and who it's for. Begin the meditation either in a seated position or lying down, but be sure that you'll be able to move around freely later on. Close your eyes and take a few deep breaths to feel the air enter and exit your lungs. As you breathe, begin to feel the lower part of your body relaxing and releasing all tension, starting with your feet. Moving upward, feel your legs and hips relax. Breathe in and feel your calves release any tension. Relax your chest and back, focus on your breathing, and allow the neck to relax and the muscles in your face and head to release as well.

Once your body is in complete relaxation, picture yourself outdoors in nature. You may be surrounded by a field or in a forest. Appreciate all the beauty of the scenery around you. Relax into a sense of comfort, calmness, and safety in this place. Focus on your root chakra at your spine's base and visualize the energy spinning in a ball, emitting a deep red color.

Take a few deep breaths and place your focus on your sacral chakra, right in the center of your lower belly and back, just below the navel. Watch the orange ball of energy swirling in you. Breathe in and focus on your solar plexus chakra near your diaphragm. Feel the energy move and spin in a yellow array.

Breathe into your heart center. Allow your heart chakra to expand into the green circle of energy. See the green color of this energy vibrate faster and faster. Pay attention to your throat chakra. Watch the shades of blue spin as they appear.

Moving upward in your body, as you breathe, focus on the energy from your third eye chakra, located between the eyebrows, and feel it grow and increase. Take a few moments to watch it, seeing its movement quicken. Visualize the crown chakra at the top of your head as the ball of white light glows, diffuses, and flows into your brain. Take a moment and enjoy the feeling of all these energy centers vibrating, churning, and pulsing energy.

Guide your attention back to your location in nature. You find a path to walk along and you are led to some steps to climb. Count them as you climb—one, two, three, four—continue counting and you arrive at a clearing.

This is where you will construct your sacred space. Use your intuition as your guide. Visualize the materials appearing as you build. Get up from your position and find some space. Go through the motions of building walls and windows. Your space may look however you like—it can be a cottage with a thatch roof, a midcentury modern house, a secret garden with ancient vines and ferns—build it however you wish it to look. This is your sacred space. You may also enter this space with the intention to find peace and clarity.

Create a door that only you will be able to enter. Imagine this as a strong door to enter and exit your space that only you have the key for. Next, create a door for others. This door is for all other entities and energies that you invite. It may be modern, electrical and made of glass, or old and ornately carved. Again, it is your preference.

Install a light above your guest door. This light will allow those who are aligned with your highest good to enter your space. The light shines bright on all who stand at the guest door of your space and serves as the gatekeeper, defending your space from anyone with ill intent.

As you finalize and finish with decorating your sacred space, take a moment to sit in it, feeling the positive energy that flows through with peace and clarity. Once you are ready and feel a state of calmness and clarity, state your intentions. Mentally or verbally call out to the archetype or to your spirit guides to give them permission to meet and state what it is you want:

> *"I wish to connect with and communicate with my spirit guides.*
> *Only energies of the light and of the highest compassion may enter.*
> *Spirit guides, I ask for your guidance.*
> *You have my gratitude and appreciation for... [name what it is you seek].*
> *In return, you have my respect, love, and devotion."*

With your eyes closed, allow for visions of a being entering through the door, coming closer to you and manifesting. Your guides will enter through your guest door into your sacred space and pass through the light. Feel the immense love as they enter. As you witness these beings coming closer through the light of the door, recognize and notice thoughts but do not follow them. Simply focus on your breath. As you remain in this receptive state, pay attention to any images, conversations, words, or sounds that occur. You may hear things in your own voice or from someone unrecognizable—listen to them and witness without force. Pay attention to your senses. What do you hear? What do you see? There may be messages provided to you.

Take a moment to enjoy your time with them and listen. Give them time to provide you with what you've asked for. When you feel you are ready to say farewell, thank them with your love, appreciation, and gratitude. You may watch them return to where they came through the guest door, or you may invite them to stay. Be absolutely sure you know who they are and what their intentions are if you ask them to stay. It is now time for you to exit your sacred place. Go through your door and shut it behind you. Walk across the clearing and down the steps back to your original location surrounded by nature. Feel your consciousness returning to your physical body, and when you are ready to wake up, open your eyes.

Now that you have created your sacred space, it can be used whenever you wish. In order to come back to it, begin by imagining sitting in a safe and comfortable place of nature. Meditate on your chakras, then follow the path and step into your space. This space can be used as a place where you can connect with your intuition, to meet loving spirits, to aid in healing, and provide you with life's answers. When you feel ready, you'll exit through your special door. Over time, your space may change in appearance; however, it will always be available to you.

Once you have cultivated a space to meet your spirit guides and build a relationship, you can easily return to your space for their love and guidance. After you have worked to build and maintain a relationship with them, you can follow the path to your special sacred place in your mind and later begin to ask your spirit guides to bring forth other spirits to communicate with you.

ASTRAL PROJECTING

Astral travel is a bit more challenging and requires more effort than pathworking. Astral travel, or spirit flight, is when you send your consciousness into the spirit world. Once you are comfortable with pathworking, can get into deep meditative states, and have mastered things like lucid dreaming, you are then ready to astral travel.

To begin, try to see your inner self that travels during meditation—it's a more transparent version of you. Visualize it lifting up and out of the physical body. This step can be challenging, but it can help you feel more connected to your etheric body. After connecting with your etheric or astral body, set a goal or destination in mind for your astral journey. This can be anything from meeting a spirit guide to exploring a place. It can also include traveling to the past or future.

Triggers are sometimes used to enter astral travel. A trigger is something to help release consciousness from the physical body. It can be found through things like music, chanting, or dancing. For instance, Shamans frequently use drumming as their triggers to achieve spirit flight. It may take many attempts to find your appropriate trigger and learn how to have control over your astral body to follow your intention. Use energetic cleansing and grounding techniques after astral projecting to avoid picking up any unwanted entities. The more you practice, the easier it becomes.

How to astral project

Before you begin, know what your goals are for your journey. Have a clear understanding, or write it down so it will be beneficial for you. Cleanse your space and use a protective item such as a piece of iron or crystal for safeguarding your physical body. This item can also help to ground your body, making it easier to find your way back to the physical plane. Go into a trance state and then disconnect from your body. If you choose to, you may call to your spirit animal for guidance or protection. When ready, return to your physical body and allow yourself to come back slowly. Finish with grounding yourself like eating or going for a short walk. You may find it helpful to record your experiences.

Animal spirit guides

Many cultures have traditions that involve the protection and guidance of an animal spirit. If you want to meet your spirit animal before embarking, make sure that you set an intention of working toward meeting your animal guide through pathworking. There are many factors to consider when choosing an animal guide. It is important to know that you aren't choosing a guide that you already know or like. Your animal guide is an important part of your spiritual journey, as they are capable of protecting and uplifting you. They may also help you in meeting other spirits or lead you to things you may need.

RITUALS

Creating a ritual can be an important step in communicating with spirits. It allows us to consciously set intentions and receive them. An intention is a way of communicating with the universe. It is like a conscious and well-considered call to action. A clear and consistent intention can serve as a reminder that you are creating. It can also serve as a guide to your path.

Intentions can be set in various ways. They can be set silently or verbally. We often set intentions all day long. Even making a list of things to do can be viewed as a basic form of intention setting. Creating a clear intention to receive certain emotions can help you experience these feelings throughout the process.

A ritual is a ceremony that involves specific actions or words. Rituals can be performed in a specific manner or can be created to a specific cultural or religious origin. With the rise of consciousness and spiritual embodiment, there has been a resurgence in the explorations of conscious rituals. A ritual is a way to set the tone and vibration of energy through various actions. A ritual that includes an intention setting helps you acknowledge and elevate your manifestation. It also communicates to the universe that you are dedicated to being a deliberate creator. A ritual can be a space of renewal and re-training, carrying the energy of commitment, integrity, and trust.

There are many ways to perform a ritual, and it's up to you to decide how you want to create it. The most basic ingredients needed are a quiet private space, a journal and pen, and being fully present. Creating a space that is designed to accommodate the ritual and its components is an important step in preparation for a powerful intention setting. Creating a ritual that allows for spontaneous action is key to your process. Be fully present in the moment—both physically and mentally. This is a time to be open to creativity and higher self-guidance. Accepting and working through difficult situations is the best way to move forward. This is also a good time to allow time and space to work through any spontaneous event that may arise. Trust that the ritual is a process that helps us to connect with our inner beings and intentions. Enjoy it as a process that helps us create powerful life experiences.

It is very important to decide what elements of your intention-setting ritual you would like to include. You can also combine elements of different rituals and add additional details as you feel called to. For instance, if you feel compelled, you may include things like divination in your rituals, or artistic movement like dancing. The choices are endless and entirely yours to customize a ritual in alignment with your intuition. It is a lot of fun to take some time to decide what elements you would like to add to your intention-setting ritual. Each ritual is powerful as it is unique and has its own unique characteristics.

Start your ritual with a clean and fresh mind and body. Wear what makes you feel powerful, comfortable, and happy. Make sure that your sacred space is clean and ready to use. This space can be sacred if you define it as a ritual space. You can purify the space with incense, or burn sage to welcome positive energy. If there are any unbeneficial energies in your space, gently ask them to leave. If you'd like your guides to assist you, you can now ask these energies to be present by including an offering or imagery at an altar. Your altar may include various items and be any layout or size you'd like. Remember, altars are about creating strong connections, and you facilitate that by placing items that are aligned with your intentions and your practice.

To start, begin centering and try deep breathing exercises to help you feel centered and connected. You can start by forming intentions in your mind as visualizations. After you have done this, speak out loud and affirm your intentions. If you choose, you may write down your intentions on a piece of paper.

Call on the energies to help you create and receive your desired changes. Remember to state within your intention how easily and positively your manifestation occurs. Express gratitude to all the elements and energies that have come to assist you. You may now close the ritual space and continue living with gratitude as the energies play out. You can also leave the space dormant and return to it periodically to work on your intentions or elements of your manifestation. There are aspects of this energy that you bring with you and can return to at any time.

OFFERINGS

There are thousands of spirits and deities, and who you choose to honor will often depend on what path you follow. Some deities are associated with specific aspects of the human experience such as love and marriage. Some spirits are associated with the phases and cycles of the planets and preside over seasons. Learning about the various types of gods and goddesses can help to identify which one would be the best fit for you to work with.

In actuality, offerings are not only for deity worship; they can be provided to all kinds of spirits, including ancestors or land spirits. Not only can offerings be used for honoring them, showing appreciation and devotion, they can also be used to pacify spirits or provide amends for accidental offense. Offerings can be provided physically or energetically and have a great power of influence or effect in gaining spiritual allies. You'll notice that physical offerings are usually still there after being given. It's rare that a spirit will have the power to consume them on the physical plane, but there are spirits who can feed off the smoke when we burn substances like plants or incense. If a physical offering is provided, such as food or drink, you can multiply its power through will with mental focus and create energetic variations.[19]

Also, offerings do not always need to be left in a ritualistic manner. They can be casually gifted and mentally provided for spirits in a plethora of settings. You may wish to recite a poem or passage that helps identify it as such. The important thing is that you make your intentions of your offering known. No matter how big or small the offering, attaching positive intent and regularly providing them will increase the chances of forming and building strong bonds with spirits.

In paganism and Wicca, practitioners may honor a god or goddess of one tradition or several. Sometimes, they may ask for help with magical tasks or in solving problems. In many traditions, it's common for people to offer a sacrifice to the gods. One of the many issues that people tend to discuss when learning about worship is the topic of proper veneration. This concept states that we should treat deities with respect and honor them appropriately when taking the time for acts of worship, like making offerings. This is not a matter of requesting and having wishes fulfilled, but rather wanting to acknowledge their existence and show how much we appreciate their influence.

---

19. Miller, Jason, *Protection & Reversal Magick: a Witch's Defense Manual* (Franklin Lakes, NJ: New Page Books, 2006), 53-55.

However, often there isn't enough clear and explicit information on a spirit's favored offering or acts of devotion. In this case, how will you know what is an appropriate offering? Deities will respond differently depending on what offering is given. This is where research is essential. For example, Athena is a goddess of war, among other things, who was born in battle armor. She is said to be enthralled by war cries. She is a powerful and primeval spirit who has been associated with Neith, an Egyptian goddess who was adopted by the Greeks and transformed into Athena after crossing the Mediterranean. She is sought for almost anything. Something related with her mythology would be appropriate offerings to consider. Offering the products of your creative effort to Athena, who is also a goddess of crafts, particularly weaving and metalworking, may be more well received than flowers, which would be better suited to a goddess of love and beauty like Aphrodite.

Learning about a spirit's or deity's myths and strengths can help to determine their preferences. It is important to consider what they represent. Aside from what the gods represent to you, it is also important that you pay attention to what they have asked of others in the past. Taking the time to learn about them shows how to worship a deity. If they represent love, for instance, what kinds of things could you offer? Examples might include roses, love letters, chocolates, candles, or incense—items that are indicative as tributes of love. When in doubt, wine and bread are often universally accepted, as well as clean water and milk. Ultimately, listen to your instincts and record what items provide you with the best response.

Chapter 12

DIVINATION

For centuries, divination tools like pendulums, runes and spirit boards have been used as methods to communicate with deceased ancestors and spirits. It wasn't until the invention of the radio and television that they were ever associated with being evil. Before this time, spiritualism and the use of divination were sought out by anyone seeking messages from the other side that inspired hope and closure. Divination is not evil, nor something to be feared, unless of course you are a person that should be feared—remember that like attracts like. Anyone who does the work for what it is intended for—to do no harm—knows that divination is simply another method to be in service for the greater good. Anyone who thinks otherwise should immediately question the origins of their beliefs. For many, divination is their preferred method to connect and communicate with spirits. Although sometimes their messages might come with difficult truths to hear, divining tools can assist in relaying messages that are incredibly powerful and healing.

Divination is a spiritual practice by definition, but it's often referred to as a methodology or an art form. The use of divinatory tools is merely an extension of spiritual communication. Practitioners combine their psychic abilities along with divinatory tools to access and interpret energetic information. The use of these tools will vary just as much as their formats. Not only are they ancient mystical tools to communicate with spirits on the other side, they can also help practitioners tap into buried knowledge of the subconscious mind or energies on other planes. Tarot and oracle cards, for example, can reveal deep-seated issues from the past, or deliver messages concerning trauma to provide insight and assist healing the benefactor. Many iterations of talking boards or spirit boards exist and are widely used, especially due to the spiritualist movement in the late nineteenth century.

However, Hollywood's depiction of divination includes far-fetched stereotypes, as well as ridiculous and unrealistic horror stories about the consequences of using a spirit or talking board. When the Kennard Novelty Company first produced the Ouija board, they had a much more lucrative initiative. Their goal was purely about making money. The use of talking boards existed centuries beforehand. It wasn't until the modern version emerged that movies like *The Exorcist* spun new ideas and beliefs about their power. The fact is, the Ouija board wasn't popularized until the patent was sold to Parker Brothers in 1966. After that, Ouija board sales rivaled the best-selling board game at the time, Monopoly.[20]

The Ouija board's history is evidence that divinatory tools are merely the means to relay spiritual messages and were used until companies patented them. It's clear that the rise of the spiritualist movement meant big business for the companies that were much more driven by lucrative-selling motives and interested in lining their pockets rather than branding the tools honestly or accurately. In other words, you may want to reconsider believing everything you see on television and social media.

The tools and practices of divination aren't restricted to the ever-popular Ouija board and tarot cards; they've been used by mediums and channelers for thousands of years, and there are hundreds of different types of divination. If you want to use divination to connect with spirits, start by deciding which one you're drawn to, which is just the one that interests you.

---

20. Edwards, Phil, "What 'Ouija' actually means, and how the game has changed," Vox, accessed Sept 22, 2020, https://www.vox.com/2015/6/11/8765053/ouija-board-meaning-name.

There is some debate on whether there are external forces manipulating divination tools on the physical plane or if a spirit is inhabiting an allotted space within us to deliver messages. If you study the difference between psychics and mediums, you'll recognize that both techniques are possible for receiving messages through divination and these two skills vary in their application as well as how information is received. Regardless of how you believe messages are delivered, you'll have a very hard time finding concrete proof that someone has been possessed simply as a result of using divination tools. These stories are unfounded, exaggerated, and no more than hearsay. It all comes down to permission and consent, like previously mentioned, stating clear boundaries and what we allow for. Now, if you simply try to reach out to any and all spirits, or tell the spirits to use your body as a vessel and give up total control over yourself, that's when you may run into precarious situations. Please don't do that. Use your common sense and don't be the idiot in a horror movie. Be clear and firm on your intentions and with whom you want to connect with to avoid these mistakes.

Divination tools can provide the means to deliver messages from spiritual planes or can help practitioners communicate energetic information from the physical plane. A medium may use divinatory tools for spirit communication, and a psychic can use the same tool for a future prediction reading. In the case of tarot cards, their application may be similar, but how the information is accessed is different. Spirits exist in different energetic planes and at different frequencies of vibration. A physical body doesn't contain their spirit, so they don't have the organs to be able to communicate with us as we do with other physical three-dimensional beings. Mediums send their consciousness to match and meet a spirit's vibrational frequency to communicate with them. A psychic, on the other hand, doesn't need to leave the physical plane to tap into psychic energy.

Certain people have a developed predisposition and gifts to intuitively recognize the messages delivered through divination. Through their use of intuition and abilities, they have the confidence to tap into energy and deliver accurate messages. It's sometimes the point of debate whether everyone can learn divination. However, I've come to find that with committed study, learning how to interpret psychic or energetic information and trusting intuition, everyone can learn how to receive accurate messages.

Although some people are more talented at certain methods of divining, just how someone can sit down at an instrument and play by ear, talent often comes in the form of being slightly more attuned to understand the mystical arts. Even so, without hard work and dedication, all talents will diminish, so don't rely on mere talent if you wish to become proficient.

The task is to figure out which form of divination appeals to you the most. This is something that may be learned by trial and error. When it comes to cartomancy, you want to choose cards that speak to you and that you are drawn to. When I first started learning to read tarot, I was told to start with the traditional Rider-Waite deck, but this advice never worked for me. What I find beneficial for divination is connecting with the instruments that I am pulled to, regardless of what guidance I receive. To this day, I can still more easily and accurately read messages using the tools that I adore.

As you begin working with your divination methods and tools, it's important to direct your questions, and not to just anyone, but address spirits by name. If you do require a bit more general audience, or don't know their name, describe who it is you're addressing so you're more likely to not potentially connect with any and every entity. Setting boundaries, like being clear on who you want to connect with, is a way of creating certainty so you can be confident who exactly it is you are talking to.

Divination is a very beneficial spiritual practice, not only in communicating with spirits. Divining has the power to establish peace and heal subconscious behaviors and traumas by allowing us to examine any deep-rooted issues in an unbiased manner. Although divination was most commonly referred to as fortune-telling and foreseeing the future, we can use these tools to access our deeper wisdom and knowing. For many practitioners, divination is a great way to begin developing intuition and accessing psychic abilities.

There are countless ways to access your gifts and begin using divination in your practice. Some methods I recommend for the beginner are through the use of books (stichomancy), cartomancy (including tarot and oracle cards), or pallomancy (the use of a pendulum). Keep in mind that these are merely tools for the practitioner. Always cleanse and shield before you begin your divination practice. Clearly direct your questions to whom you wish to answer them. It's up to you whether you choose to clear or banish when you are finished with them. As I've mentioned before, if you invite energies and entities to stick around, be absolutely sure you know who and what it is. Spirit guides are always a good idea to begin with asking for assistance.

Each divination method has its own strengths and weaknesses, so you may choose to combine different types of divination methods to get more clarity in readings. If you aren't receiving a clear answer, you may need to rephrase the question. In the case of a pendulum, you are limited to asking only yes and no questions. The same goes for books, runes, and tarot cards—answers can be limited by the tools you use.

Begin by simply explaining what is directly provided for more accurate readings. Do not attempt to interpret the messages immediately. After you've studied your preferred way to fully comprehend the communication, keep in mind that the tools are there to assist you in accessing the knowledge, not to generate it. In the case of future predictions, the messages delivered are merely a direction established on the present road and are susceptible to change because time is not linear and nothing is fixed in stone.

STICHOMANCY

Stichomancy is one of the oldest forms of divination. Some sources suggest that it dates back thousands of years. Stichomancy is a type of divination that uses a random passage from a book. This method helps to bring clarity to a situation. A reading can be done when there are a variety of books in one area. If you don't have your own bookshelf, this can be done at a library or bookstore.

To perform a stichomancy reading, close your eyes and think about a question. Extend your arm forward and point, then follow your pointing finger and pick the book that calls to you. Flip through the pages of the book and open to a page once you feel you should stop, keep your eyes closed, and point at a random spot on the page. Open them and read the passage you've pointed to. Use your intuition to interpret the passage.

CARTOMANCY

The most common misconceptions about tarot are that it opens a portal to the spirit world and that it is more than just a playing card. In fact, it originated from a medieval Italian game called Tarocchi. The use of archetypes in tarot cards helps readers identify the patterns and hidden influences that lay beneath their ordinary circumstances. Most tarot decks follow the same basic set of symbols and traditional meanings. This means that new readers will need to learn the accepted meanings in order to successfully read tarot.

Oracle cards have been gaining popularity in the New Age and witchcraft communities in the last couple of years. One of their biggest characteristics is their variety, which makes them so versatile. Some readers also find that oracle cards give more surface-level information. Another common complaint about Oracle cards is that they tend to be overwhelmingly positive. This is also true for many decks, which tend to shy away from darker themes. Finding a balanced deck can help avoid focusing too much on the positive. Though oracle cards are very useful for beginners, they're also great for experienced users. Ultimately, the best way to find a good deck is to find one that you have a strong attraction to.

Divination, like all spiritual practices, is a very personal experience. To begin, start off with clearing and cleansing. For this, I usually light incense. Follow this by centering. The last thing I do before a reading is set the intention of who I want to connect with. For example, I would say, "I am asking to connect with my spirits guides of the highest love and compassion." Then ask your question as you shuffle or scan the cards. If you are reading for someone else, ask the person what question they'd like answered, and then you can have them select which cards they feel drawn to.

In order to choose a card, you may feel drawn to certain cards like a magnet. This is especially apparent if the cards are fanned out. Your fingers may act like a magnet and get pulled to the correct card. If you're shuffling and receive cards that fly out of the deck, they are often referred to as jump cards.

In this instance you know that's a message that must be heard immediately. Cards that are drawn or jump out may contain the answer to your question, or might be an important message that is urgent.

The methods to select cards are endless, as well as the number of spreads you set your intention with. Follow your gut instinct and intuition. You will need to learn to trust what intuitive nudges you're getting in order to receive an accurate message. This is why people who have developed either psychic abilities or mediumship can better understand when a message is the right one.

When you get a card deck, it's important to connect with it. You can do this several ways. Some practitioners carry their decks around with them for a few days or even weeks. Some even sleep next to them. Essentially you're infusing your energy with a deck so that you're connected to it. So connect with your cards. I always interview a deck because I feel each deck is unique, and I use them for different kinds of information and guidance. So if you're like me and you get a new deck and want to interview it to understand it better and connect with it, here's a spread you can use:

Card Deck Interview Spread

You will need to shuffle and draw six cards. The card spread will be placed in two rows of three, with three cards above and three cards below. Set your intention and ask the following questions as you pull each card.

Top left card: *What is the overall energy of this deck?*
Top center card: *What are your strengths as a deck?*
Top right card: *What are your limits as a deck?*
Bottom left card: *What are you here to teach me?*
Bottom center card: *How can I best learn from you?*
Bottom right card: *What is the potential outcome of working with this deck?*

A note on card reading: while all decks come with guidebooks, I recommend looking at the card and attempting to decipher the message based on the artwork. If you understand numerology, the card's number can also play a vital role. The number one is frequently connected with beginnings, whereas ten is typically associated with completion. Before or during your shuffle, identify your intention, state your boundaries of who is allowed to connect, and ask a question.

Tarot cards are divided into two categories: the major and minor arcana. For the minor arcana, the suit holds significant meaning as well. Swords are associated with the element air and represent thoughts or the mind. Cups are symbolized with water to represent emotion or the heart. Wands are connected to the element fire and represent action or movement. And coins, pentacles, or disks represent the element earth and the physical or material world.

PALLOMANCY

A pendulum is a small, weighted object that hangs from a string or chain. You can buy one specifically made for divination, or you can also use anything that you already own, like a necklace. If you've never used one before, you can easily use it on your own.

To begin using a pendulum, hold it in your hands and practice feeling connected to it. From there, let it swing freely and ask it to confirm its motion for yes, then stop it and ask it to confirm its motion for no. This may be different for everyone. Even some pendulums owned by the same practitioner may show different motions for yes or no. Once you have confirmation on the meaning of its motion, you can begin asking questions.

A pendulum is also a useful tool for getting clarification on previous readings from other divination methods. The downside to pendulum readings is that they can answer only simple yes or no questions. This means that they can be used only for specific inquiries. They are also not the best tool for general readings or open-ended guidance.

For accurate readings, begin by administering your cleansing and protection methods. Center and clear your mind. Once calm, clear, and ready, and the pendulum is at a full stop, ask a yes or no question. When complete, express your appreciation for the guidance, and ground yourself with your preferred method.

Chapter 13

INVOCATION VERSUS EVOCATION

Formal ceremonies and rituals are usually part of invocation and evocation. However, we can invite specific archetypes, spirits, entities, and deities into our lives to aid us with our intentions without lengthy and complicated rituals. The types of energies, entities, and archetypes that we may call upon for assistance vary—they can be spiritual, cultural, or religious. For example, you may call upon Archangel Michael to help guide your visions and intentions into the earth realm. Perhaps if you are working on manifesting wealth, you may wish to call upon the energy of the Greek God Plutus or Hindu Goddess Lakshmi to assist you.

It may be difficult to recognize the difference between invocation and evocation, but understanding the difference between the terminology will help in understanding how to perform them and can give practitioners the necessary knowledge to bolster their practice. Both invoking and evoking refer to summoning spirits; to the novice, it may seem as though the words are interchangeable. However, if we dive deeper into the etymology of the two words, we begin to recognize their differences and applications.

Invoking contains the word "in" and references connecting to, meeting, or drawing a spirit within ourselves.[21] The word "invocation" derives from

---

21. McCabe, Samuel, "Invocation vs. Evocation," RitualCravt: Metaphysical & Witchy Wares, accessed April 30, 2021, https://www.ritualcravt.com/invocation-vs-evocation/.

the Latin word *invocare*, which means "to summon down from above," or "to bring a spirit into one's self." Practitioners who invoke spirits do so with the intention of meeting the spirit within themselves for direction or support, rather than calling for a spirit to materialize on this plane at a specific location. Evocation differs as it means to "call out" or "call from." The word "evocation" derives from the Latin *evocare*, which means "to summon a spirit from beyond oneself."[22] Evoking is a process that is external. From here, we begin to recognize how invocation differs from evocation. Invoking spirits is to call upon their energy to come within and bring a sense of support and detail, as opposed to evocation—to call forth a spirit from their plane of existence with an external involvement.

Calling forth a spirit might seem fairly intricate and difficult, but it is surprisingly easy, consisting of only five procedures or phases. There are many ways to informally invoke spirits, but formal evocation has five steps, and invocation only has three, and they both share the first two. These five stages include consecration, invocation, confining, binding, and releasing. The invocation employs the first two phases plus a communion, while evocation uses all five.

A length of time would be required to focus, imagine, sacralize the conjuration site, and then prepare for the actual conjuration. The summoning takes place at a set time within a sanctified holy area that has been formed by purifications and ceremonial offerings, and then a circular barrier is drawn.

The usage of pots of water or dirt, iron chains, and brass containers were all used to capture and bind spirits. Spirits might be bound and imprisoned in a metal bottle, similar to the *Arabian Nights*' brass lamp harboring a strong djinni. Focusing and accepting the spirit when it came was constraining, while binding was attaching it to a specific work or goal. An agreement, treaty, or offer might also be included. Giving the spirit permission to leave was referred to as releasing.

Spirits can be called forth in a number of ways, such as through cer-

22. Barrabbas, Frater, *Spirit Conjuring for Witches: Magical Evocation Simplified* (Woodbury, MN: Llewellyn Worldwide Ltd, 2017), 22.

emonial magic. The purpose here is to highlight the distinction between invocation and evocation rather than to teach ceremonial magic. Because I don't employ formal methods of ceremonial magic to conjure spirits, I'm not going to describe a step-by-step approach. If that's the way that resonates with you and that you like, there are other more trained practicing ceremonial magicians who can provide it better. There are several resources available if you like ceremonial magic. I only discuss invocation in the context of ceremonial magic so that you may get a sense of the various avenues you might take to engage with spirits and explore what resonates with you. In my experience, casual invocations and other terms for the technique have worked for me once I've had a strong connection and established a dynamic relationship with a spirit. Here are some instances of informal applications, which are simpler ways.

Informal invocations can be recited in affirmations, songs, or poems. This is generally a passage that calls the spirit to connect within you. The options are endless; it can be a prayer, a hymn, an affirmation, or a poem. If you wish to invoke an ancestor, for instance, state your intention by reciting their favorite song lyrics, or reading aloud from a favorite novel.

Informal evocations of a spirit can be done by simply addressing it and inviting it to join you in a ritual or activity. Sometimes it's as simple as providing an offering in the hopes that the deity would appear. Whatever the case may be, evoking is an exterior interaction with the spirit. In any event, before bringing a spirit into your life be sure they are well-known and trustworthy.

Certain substances may also assist with rituals for some individuals. Wine, for example, may be featured in numerous invocation rites from various civilizations. Some scents are said to help with psychic ability or the capacity to sense spirits. Botanical scents like lilac, rosemary, and wisteria are examples. Myrrh's scent is thought to open doors to spirit realms. Remember to investigate what is suitable for the spirit you are calling before using any ritual element. Calling spirits into your life ultimately is about connecting with your heart in order to form a functional and productive connection.

So far, we've learned little about the mechanics of invocation. Remember, I mentioned that invocation is a method of voluntary spirit possession. First and foremost, you can only be vague at best when characterizing anything that unites the physical, esoteric, cosmic, and theological domains.

Spirit assumption is viewed by some in the neo-pagan culture as a collection of different experiences related to different levels of the spirit's presence. Authors and practitioners Kenaz Filan and Raven Kaldera initiated and skilled in shamanic and vodou traditions, ascribed an initial list to Willow Polson, and added to it in terms of spiritual presence stages.[23]

Enhance

Giving a third-person invocation or recounting a tale are examples. As a result, people's understanding of that spirit, their immediate connection with them, and their sensation of presence at the event *enhance*. All that is necessary for improvement is knowledge of the spirit rather than any type of interaction with them. As an example, as part of a rite, a priestess relates the narrative of Athena's birth in such a manner that people remember the statue of Athena dressed in battle gear and what that signified.

Inspire

In the sense that you're offering an invocation or narrating a story, this is comparable to enhancement, but the distinction is that with inspiration you're speaking from the spirit's perspective. You talk for others rather than for yourself in this situation. "Athena desires this," rather than "Athena accomplished this." The two parts of inspiration are knowing who the spirit is and imagining what they would desire.

Integrate

Integration takes it a step further by allowing you to speak in the first person as the spirit. This is usually reserved for the ritual's high point.

---

23. Filan, Kenaz, and Kaldera, Raven, *Drawing Down the Spirits* (Rochester, Vermont: Inner Traditions International, 2009), 158-162.

The traditional Wiccan "drawing down the Moon," in which the high priestess appears and talks as if she were the goddess herself, is an example of this. "I am the green earth's beauty, the white moon amid the stars, and the enigma of the seas..." In some ways, it's as if you're transforming yourself into a devotional figure for the spirit.

Aspect

The human being in charge has been in complete control of the situation up to this point on the list, and the presence of the deity as an entity may not even be present. Enhancement, inspiration, and integration can all be done without having an astral link to the god or goddess you're honoring, but aspecting takes you to a higher level when the spirit is engaged. From this point on, the human being's choices and control become less significant, while the spirit's choices and control grow more essential. Without the active involvement of the entity in question, progress is difficult to impossible. Of course, the spirit can intervene at any of the three steps already mentioned and create a relationship; two-way contact can occur spontaneously. Inspiration might turn into channeling all of a sudden.

When someone is aspected, they are a complete channel for the spirit's energy and frequently their words, but the spirit has not totally taken over the flesh body to walk around in it and consider it as their own. The individual is acting as a conduit for their energy rather than their physical presence. Some call this "co-consciousness," which implies that the spirit's intellect and energy, as well as their own, are both present and share command of what will be uttered. People who have never dealt with full-on possession sometimes confuse aspecting with it. Many individuals can aspect a spirit they can't completely horse, and aspecting is far less taxing and gentler on the body and spirit. The term 'horse' is used in reference to spiritual possession as a metaphor to describe when a spirit is essentially riding a person's physical body. In this case the spirit is in control of a person's movements and actions as long as the person remains passive and allows for the spirit's control. The experience can be terminated by the horse at any point.

Shadow

As many people have phrased it, this is when the spirits "ride along in your mind." There's a sense that they're just behind your shoulder, able to communicate plainly to you (and some may even have a running commentary going during a shadowing experience), but they're not utilizing your body. You're in complete control of your reactions. You can "take dictation" and convey their remarks, or you can reword them, or you can remain mute depending on the scenario. Shadowing can occur as a personal experience (for example, when you're going through the mall and your matron goddess tells you which item they want you to buy for them), or as part of a ritual or spiritual counseling; in the latter instance, it can turn into channeling.

Channel

Channeling, popularized by New Agers, is a type of partial possession in which an entity is permitted to utilize a human's voice or hands but does not actively take over the entire body. Because there is more of a relationship between the channel and the "guest," this is more prevalent with "lesser," non-divine spirits. Although this is not a hard-and-fast rule, deities are more likely to desire to take over the entire body. If there isn't enough connection, some people may resort to channeling, or letting go on the horse's part to handle complete possession.

Possess

The spirit enters the person's body, temporarily displacing their own consciousness, and talks directly to the audience or client in this moment, which is the greatest connection of all. The spirit may also hijack the body for various purposes, depending on the spirit and the scenario. The horse's consciousness is either extremely distant (horses have reported seeing and hearing things as if underwater or from a great distance away, in a very dissociative manner, or the sound may be turned off entirely) or completely unconscious at this point.

Chapter 14

THE DIFFERENCE BETWEEN
PSYCHICS AND MEDIUMS

All mediums are psychic but not all psychics are mediums. Psychics and mediums both utilize the clair senses to acquire their information or messages. Some will acquire intuitive knowledge in the form of feeling or knowing, which is known as clairsentience and claircognizance. In other circumstances, they may be able to see images or visual communications, which is known as clairvoyance. They can also experience hearing messages known as clairaudience. Psychic taste and smell are referred to as clairgustance and clairessence, also known as clairalience and clairolfaction. Most psychics and mediums will usually have one or two dominant clair senses that are strongest, and so they have to work on developing other senses if they want to use them. Inherent psychic abilities will depend on your genetics, and the rest can be developed.

The difference between psychics and mediums is how they receive and interact with subtle energy. Mediums are people who send their consciousness to meet spirits. Spirits exist energetically on a much higher vibrational frequency. In order to meet them, mediums must raise their vibration and the spirit will generally have to slow down. Mediums usually have a calling to be of service in some way for people. Psychics, however, tend to operate with energy on the earthly plane. A psychic doesn't need to connect with the energy of a spirit or access any of the spiritual realms to be psychic.

What makes them psychic is the ability to access and interpret the energy or information that is concealed from the conventional senses. Their abilities can free them from the rules of time and space.

Therefore, a medium is someone who uses their psychic skills to contact and speak with spirits. Psychics, on the other hand, use extrasensory perception to detect information that is concealed from the ordinary senses. Although it is possible to learn to access the spiritual realm, most mediums must increase their awareness and knowledge of the energy information they receive. Psychics and mediums both need to be skilled communicators. Nevertheless, some psychics require little or no preparation in order to put their abilities to use. The challenge often resides in deciphering, interpreting, and translating the information so we can understand it. Ultimately if you don't want to be of service, that's okay. Perhaps you just wish to strengthen your psychic abilities or mediumship skills in order to improve your communication with departed loved ones or your guides. To begin, we must comprehend how psychics and mediums receive energetic information, as well as the differences between psychic activity and mediumship.

PSYCHICS

Everyone has some innate psychic talent, and enhancing yours can be an exercise of self-awareness. Meditation is one of the most effective methods for developing psychic abilities since it allows us to access our subconscious and all of its contents.

The aura seems to be what determines how we read people psychically. By reaching out to another person's auric field, psychics can tune in to the information of energy. An aura is the magnetic energy, or energy field, surrounding all living things. It contains our thoughts, memories, emotions, and experiences. This is how psychic readings are performed, by tapping into the information of another person's aura.

Psychics link to the auric fields of others by extending out energetically, like two tentacles of energy joining. High-vibration emotions like joy and love expand the auric field, and low-vibration emotion, such as hate or anger, can shrink it. Our memories and emotions are held inside the aura's energy. Colors can be seen in the aura by certain psychics. The colors of someone's aura can be read by a good psychic. We may not be able to see the colors when we connect with someone, but we certainly sense them. Working with color in a way that suits your values, customs, and culture is a good way to strengthen your skills.

You may detect your psychic gifts, also known as the clair senses, by your intuitive responses to people. Have trust in it and believe in yourself. When operating psychically or through mediumship, we must acquire the language in order to interpret. We must then interpret it for the person for whom we are doing the reading. Mediums and psychics must be excellent communicators. Psychically, comparable or shared experiences are simpler to perceive and describe. You can be sure you'll notice it. The more you practice, the more you can learn to distinguish between what you're picking up and what energy is your own. Acknowledge symbols and feel into what you are receiving. As you offer for the recipient, more will emerge. Interpret the situation as best you can.

Recognize that psychic energy tends to come from a forward direction, as if you are energetically drawing information toward you. Recognize when your logical mind enters the picture. With a rational mind, your psychic skills will not function effectively. Remember that connecting in a group situation is more challenging. It's simpler to connect with the proper individual when you're working one-on-one. The importance of intention cannot be overstated! Set boundaries and be explicit about what you're doing.

Try feeling your auric field to improve your psychic abilities. Visualize the energy coming up from the Earth's core, engulfing you in a dazzling beam of light. Through the solar plexus, inhale vital energy and feel your intentions shoot out. Visualize and feel your aura growing. Create the energetic space to tap into another's auric field with their consent. Try to figure out who they are.

Take control of your situation. Relax. Concentrate on your breathing. Allow it to establish its own rhythm. Feel the location of the energy.

Recognize yourself. Set aside your rational thought process. It should be placed on a shelf.

Try to sense a psychic pull from yourself to them. Connect with them by visualizing some of your aura holding on to theirs. Take note of the information in front of you. Psychic knowledge is present in the space of a half moon in front of you. This energy information is frequently quite visible in the mind's eye, or elicits powerful emotions. Make an emotional connection with them. Recognize their individuality. After that, we may perceive words, images, sensations, and emotions.

MEDIUMS

Mediums get messages from the spiritual worlds and in a number of ways. The phrases "vital body" and "vital forces" are commonly used in the spiritual community. The vital body is another way of referring to the soul. It is the invincible eternal power that is inside each of us. Our vital body is, in truth, more real than our physical body. The air contains vital forces that can boost our energy. As mediums, we must connect with these key elements in order to increase our vibration to a level where we can communicate with spirits.

We perceive spirits with our clair senses. The energetic information is then interpreted by our brain so we can explain what we feel, smell, taste, see, or hear. Our consciousness works in connection with our brain. The right side of the brain, or the creative and imaginative part, is crucial and a key component for mediumship. The left side of the brain, the logical mind, destroys the experience of mediumship. We need to subdue the logic and keep the creative mind aware. In other words, we need to be open to believing. The easiest way to remain open is to move into a daydreamer mode—aware, but not fully present.

As mediums, our bubble of energy needs to coincide with a spirit's. When we build and sit in the power, we create a space to interact with spirits. In order to get to this stage, mediums go through a meditative and centering practice often referred to as "building the power." To build the power is to increase the vital energy in the vital body. Mediums will often experience or feel like the information and connection comes from a specific area of space. For example, when I connect with spirits, I often feel them from behind, like a loving embrace or a hand on the shoulder. The experience is always a very positive one. It's important to allow the experience flow and follow the information without force.

The vital energy is limitless, there is an endless supply of it. But psychics and mediums can get tired and drained, just like an athlete on a treadmill, because it's not our natural state. Reaching spiritual realms can be exhausting. Rest and recuperation are important. We can drain our psychic energy. Listen to what your body needs.

Building & Moving into the Power Exercise

It's crucial to remember why you want to communicate with spirits before you begin. Positive effects will be ensured by pure intents of assisting and healing. This meditation may be performed easily to get access to and enter the light, allowing you to receive accurate messages from spirit. Before commencing this meditation, it's critical that you follow the prior exercises to ensure that it's successful, that you understand how spirits communicate, and that you maintain your light.

Set your intention once you're ready to make room for spirit. As you begin to concentrate on your breathing, get comfortable. Start this meditation by lighting a candle, burning incense, or holding a crystal. Then, to generate calm, clear your thoughts and bring your awareness to the present now, focus on your breath. As you inhale and exhale, notice how your breath feels in your body.

As you breathe in and out, notice where your body expands and contracts. Longer exhales bring your thoughts back to the present moment and create a stillness or empty space in front of you. Allow ideas to enter your mind, recognize them, and then just let them go, returning your attention to your breathing.

Begin to elevate your vibration by picturing happy memories and feeling thankful for the things and people you care about. The next stage is to charge your chakras with the vital energy that surrounds us so that you may send your energy to the farthest reaches of the cosmos. Visualize the center and core of the Earth's energy. Imagine it rising to the surface and encompassing you in its electric and revitalizing energy. As it moves up your body, begin with your root chakra at the base of the spine and visualize the vital energy feeding and lighting it up. Visualize the vital energy moving up and doing the same for the sacral chakra igniting an orange color below the navel, and igniting the solar plexus chakra with yellow below the chest. As it moves up it ignites your heart chakra with green light and continues upward to the throat chakra, igniting a brilliant blue color. Then it continues up to the third eye as it illuminates a brilliant purple between your eyebrows, and continues to the crown chakra at the top of the head where you see a brilliant white light. Take a minute to submit to the experience and envision putting your ego or rational mind on a shelf as you conduct this exercise. Realize now that you are boundless. Push out all your energy as far as you can. Send it up and out in a burst of energy through the cosmos and universe. Visualize it emanating and pulsing huge amounts from your spiritual body. Send your light up and out.

Roll your eyes upward to the back of your head to envision your consciousness coming out of you and up. Imagine this as an elevator ride into the void, to a new dimension of reality, to a realm of oneness, pleasure, joy, and love.

Feel the energy shift and change, such as a ringing in the ears, body tingles, or maybe a lightness in the air and atmosphere. Step into that light. Everyone experiences what the shift is like differently. Once you feel present and sense a stillness for clarity, ask your spirit guides to come close. Say, *"Spirit guides of the highest love and compassion, I ask for your assistance. Please come close."*

Feel your consciousness come back into your body. At this time you may sit with your spirit guide and ask them any questions you might have, or if you are working with a sitter—a person you are providing mediumship for—you may ask your spirit guide to retrieve a deceased person with a message and relay it to you. If you wish to have your spirit guide retrieve a deceased person for your sitter, or for the person you are reading for, your request may sound like this:

Say to spirit, *"I would like you to bring somebody who's passed over with a message for [name]."*

Do not fear these spirits that are being retrieved. Your spirit guides will bring only those with an important message who mean no harm. Feel intuitively what messages you are receiving. What do you hear, feel, or see?

Give your love and gratitude as you say farewell to the spirits as a form of respect. Your light is pure love. Energetically connect and cultivate that love for strong and powerful connections.

To review:
 • Cultivate the space for spirits through your breath work.
 • Set your intention.
 • Send out your energy.
 • Own it, practice it, step into it.
 • Ask your spirit guide to come close.
 • Thank the spirits with love and gratitude.

Your connection will get stronger with time and your relationship with spirits will improve. Recognize the goal to build and develop a safe, sacred space, as well as the stillness in front of you to facilitate communication. Request that your spirit team join you in forming an alliance and forming a partnership. Send out your energy as a bright light, and express your objectives clearly to spirits so they know what they need to accomplish.

Guides are a collective awareness that manifests in many forms to assist us in identifying them. The vital energy may be used whenever you need to replenish. Simply be aware of it and allow it to heal. We're on a journey of learning, therefore we'll need to take our time. Get to know the members of your spirit team. Guides have a very personal relationship with us. They may only resonate with you because of their appearance or attributes. They can appear in many forms including humans, animals, or cosmic beings. Guides can advise us on our abilities. They can assist us in gaining confidence. You'll be able to discern whether anything is accurate if you ask your guides for validation and proof, which they will provide in the form of signs or synchronicities regarding what they tell you or show you.

As you work with spirits, allow for the spirit to tell you. You can't compel information with your rational mind. Have faith that it will occur. Feel your way through symbols and visuals. If you're working with a sitter, you can begin describing what you're sensing with prompts like "It feels like…" or "I'm starting to see that…" to start articulating what you're feeling. Take advantage of your strongest clair senses by being aware of them. Your confirmations will gradually educate you which information is correct. We learn by doing. Mediumship is like learning a new language.

BIBLIOGRAPHY

Abel, C. "The Duality, Paradox, and Harmony behind the YinYang." Medium. Accessed May 20, 2020. https://medium.com/the-philosophers-stone/symbology-of-symbols-the-yinyang-7da94af198a6.

Andrews, Ted. *How To Meet and Work With Spirit Guides*. 2nd ed. Woodbury, MN: Llewellyn Publications, 2006.

Aulinas, Anna. "Physiology Of The Pineal Gland And Melatonin." Ncbi. Nlm.Nih.Gov, https://www.ncbi.nlm.nih.gov/books/NBK550972/.

Auryn, Mat. *Psychic Witch: a Metaphysical Guide to Meditation, Magick & Manifestation*. Woodbury, MN: Llewellyn Worldwide Ltd, 2020.

Barrabbas, Frater. *Spirit Conjuring for Witches: Magical Evocation Simplified*. Woodbury, MN: Llewellyn Worldwide Ltd, 2017.

Brand, Damon. *Magickal Protection: Defend Against Curses, Gossip, Bullies, Thieves, Demonic Forces, Violence, Threats And Psychic Attack*. Scotts Valley, CA: Createspace Independent Publishing Platform, 2015.

Buckland, Raymond. *Buckland's Book of Spirit Communications*. Woodbury, MN: Llewellyn, 2008.

Coleman, Martin. *Communing with the Spirits: the Magical Practice of Necromancy Simply and Lucidly Explained, with Full Instructions for the Practice of That Ancient Art*. Philadelphia, PA: Xlibris, 2005.

Colosimo, Natalie. "Elementals and Earth Spirits." The Psychic School. Accessed Oct 20, 2021. https://psychicschool.com/elementals-and-earth-spirits.

DuQuette, Lon Milo. *Low Magick: It's All in Your Head, You Just Have No Idea How Big Your Head Is.* Woodbury, MN: Llewellyn Publications, 2010.

Edwards, Phil. "What 'Ouija' actually means, and how the game has changed." Vox. Accessed Sept 22, 2020. https://www.vox.com/2015/6/11/8765053/ouija-board-meaning-name.

Faeriepedia. "A Hitchhiker's Guide to Faerie." Accessed Jun 12, 2020. https://faeriepedia.weebly.com/a-hitchhikers-guide-to-faerie.html.

Filan, Kenaz and Kaldera, Raven. *Drawing Down the Spirits.* Rochester, Vermont: Inner Traditions International, 2009.

Grimassi, Raven. *Encyclopedia of Wicca & Witchcraft.* Woodbury, MN: Llewellyn, 2007.

Harper, Douglas. "Etymology of demon." Online Etymology Dictionary. Accessed Nov 19, 2021. https://www.etymonline.com/word/demon.

Illes, Judika. *Encyclopedia Of Spirits.* New York, NY: HarperCollins Publishers, 2009.

Kelden. *The Crooked Path: An Introduction to Traditional Witchcraft.* Woodbury, MN: Llewellyn Worldwide Ltd., 2020.

Konstantinos. *Summoning Spirits: the Art of Magical Evocation.* Woodbury, MN: Llewellyn Publications, 2009.

Kraig, Donald M. "Lesser Banishing Ritual of the Pentagram." Llewellyn Worldwide. Accessed Jul 21, 2005. https://www.llewellyn.com/encyclopedia/article/5139.

Lysette, Chantel. *The Angel Code: Your Interactive Guide to Angelic Communication.* Woodbury, MN: Llewellyn Publications, 2010.

McCabe, Samuel. "Invocation vs. Evocation." RitualCravt: Metaphysical & Witchy Wares. Accessed Apr 30, 2021. https://www.ritualcravt.com/invocation-vs-evocation.

Miller, Jason. *Protection & Reversal Magick: a Witch's Defense Manual.* Franklin Lakes, NJ: New Page Books, 2006.

Morrison, Dorothy. *Utterly Wicked: Hexes, Curses, and Other Unsavory Notions*. York Beach, ME: Weiser, 2020.

Nathaniel. *The Art of Seeing Your Psychic Intuition, Third Eye, and Clairvoyance: A Practical Manual for Learning and Improving Your Clairvoyant Abilities*. Wrocław, Poland: A State of Mind, 2012.

Oberon, Aaron. *Southern Cunning: Folkloric Witchcraft in the American South*. Winchester, England: Moon Books, 2019.

Peterson, Joseph H. *Arbatel: Concerning The Magic Of The Ancients*. Lake Worth, FL: Ibis Press, 2009.

Pullman, Philip. *His Dark Materials: Northern Lights*. London, UK: Scholastic, 1995.

Sam. "Everything You Need To Know About Pagan Deity (Paganism 101)." The Illuminated Witch. Accessed Mar 21, 2021. https://theilluminatedwitch.wordpress.com/2021/03/26/everything-you-need-to-know-about-pagan-deity-paganism-101.

———. "The Little Gods: Spirits Of Place In Modern Paganism (Paganism 101)." The Illuminated Witch. Accessed Jun 30, 2021. https://theilluminatedwitch.wordpress.com/2021/05/23/the-little-gods.

———. "Working with Spirits (Baby Witch Bootcamp Ch. 17)." The Illuminated Witch. Accessed Jun 30, 2021. https://theilluminatedwitch.wordpress.com/2020/07/28/working-with-spirits-baby-witch-bootcamp-ch-17.

Trank, Lisa. "These Ancient Symbols Were Believed To Offer Protection From Harm." Gaia. Accessed Jan 23, 2021. https://www.gaia.com/article/ancient-symbols-of-protection-from-around-the-world.

Wagner, Paul. "Are You A Starseed? Read These 27 Starseed Characteristics." Gaia. Accessed Nov 15, 2020. https://www.gaia.com/article/am-i-a-starseed-types-characteristics.

Weschcke, Carl L. "The Goal of High Magick is Initiation." Llewellyn Worldwide. Accessed Feb 22, 2021, https://www.llewellyn.com/encyclopedia/article/25576.

Wigington, Patti. "Magical Grounding, Centering, and Shielding Techniques." Learn Religions. Accessed Mar 30, 2021. https://www.learnreligions.com/grounding-centering-and-shielding-4122187.

————."Pagan Gods and Goddesses." Learn Religions. Jun 18, 2021, https://www.learnreligions.com/pagan-gods-and-goddesses-2561985.

————."What is a Psychic Medium?" Learn Religions. Accessed Nov 15, 2021. https://www.learnreligions.com/what-is-a-medium-2561904.

————."7 Ways to Develop Your Psychic Abilities." Learn Religions. Accessed Nov 16, 2021. https://www.learnreligions.com/ways-to-develop-your-psychic-abilities-2561759.

Made in the USA
Monee, IL
25 April 2023

818df810-31f2-44e9-89e1-9cc67ac27e09R01